REA's Test Prep Books Are The Best!

(a sample of the <u>hundreds of letters</u> REA receives each year)

(more on next page)

D1406476

(continued from front page)

" I just wanted to thank you for helping me get a great score
on the AP U.S. History... Thank you for making great test preps! "
Student, Los Angeles, CA

" Your *Fundamentals of Engineering Exam* book was the absolute best
preparation I could have had for the exam, and it is one of the major
reasons I did so well and passed the FE on my first try. "
Student, Sweetwater, TN

" I used your book to prepare for the test and found that the advice and the
sample tests were highly relevant... Without using any other material, I earned
very high scores and will be going to the graduate school of my choice. "
Student, New Orleans, LA

" What I found in your book was a wealth of information sufficient to shore up
my basic skills in math and verbal... The section on analytical ability was
excellent. The practice tests were challenging and the answer explanations
most helpful. It certainly is the Best Test Prep for the GRE! "
Student, Pullman, WA

" I really appreciate the help from your excellent book. Please keep
up with your great work."
Student, Albuquerque, NM

" I used your *CLEP Introductory Sociology* book and rank it 99% — thank you! "
Student, Jerusalem, Israel

" The painstakingly detailed answers in the sample tests are the most helpful
part of this book. That's one of the great things about REA books. "
Student, Valley Stream, NY

(more on back page)

The Best Test Preparation for the
NEW JERSEY
HSPA

High School Proficiency Assessment in

Language Arts

by the Staff of
Research & Education Association

Research & Education Association
61 Ethel Road West
Piscataway, New Jersey 08854

**The Best Test Preparation for the
New Jersey HSPA in Language Arts**

Year 2005 Printing

Printed in the United States of America

Library of Congress Control Number 2003090660

International Standard Book Number 0-87891-460-9

REA® is a registered trademark of Research & Education Association, Inc., Piscataway, New Jersey 08854.

A Message to Educators and Students

All New Jersey students are required to pass all sections of the HSPA before they can graduate high school. The state-administered Alternate Proficiency Assessment may be used to evaluate whether or not a student has attained proficiency in the necessary skills if he or she does not pass the HSPA.

The HSPA is not an easy test to pass. It was designed to be more challenging than the state's previous high school exit exam, the HSPT.

It is important, therefore, that students extensively review the subjects covered by the HSPA, and become well acquainted with the types of questions that can be expected to be on the test.

This book is arranged to help students pass the Language Arts section of the HSPA by providing:

1. An individual study plan and guidance to help students concentrate on subject areas that they need to work on most when preparing for the exam.

2. **Two** full-length practice exams based on the format of the most recent exams given.

3. Types of questions likely to be on the exam.

4. A **full and detailed explanation** of the answer to each exam question.

5. Comprehensive reviews of all subjects covered on the exam.

NOTE TO EDUCATORS:

A large number of class and homework assignments that may be assigned to students are included at the back of the book. Answers to the assigned questions are given in the Teacher's Guide, which is available from REA.

TABLE OF CONTENTS

About Research & Education Association

Founded in 1959, Research & Education Association is dedicated to publishing the finest and most effective educational materials—including software, study guides, and test preps—for students in middle school, high school, college, graduate school, and beyond.

REA's Test Preparation series includes study guides for all academic levels in almost all disciplines. Research & Education Association publishes test preps for students who have not yet completed high school, as well as high school students preparing to enter college. Students from countries around the world seeking to attend college in the United States will find the assistance they need in REA's publications. For college students seeking advanced degrees, REA publishes test preps for many major graduate school admission examinations in a wide variety of disciplines, including engineering, law, and medicine. Students at every level, in every field, with every ambition can find what they are looking for among REA's publications.

Unlike most test preparation books—which present only a few practice tests that bear little resemblance to the actual exams—REA's series presents tests that accurately depict the official exams in both degree of difficulty and types of questions. REA's practice tests are always based upon the most recently administered exams, and include every type of question that can be expected on the actual exams.

REA's publications and educational materials are highly regarded and continually receive an unprecedented amount of praise from professionals, instructors, librarians, parents, and students. Our authors are as diverse as the fields represented in the books we publish. They are well-known in their respective disciplines and serve on the faculties of prestigious high schools, colleges, and universities throughout the United States and Canada.

Acknowledgments

We would like to thank Larry B. Kling, Manager, Editorial Services, for his editorial direction; Rob Coover, Associate Editor, for managing development of this title; Anita Price Davis of Converse College and Brian Walsh of Rutgers University for their editorial contributions; and Wende Solano for typesetting the manuscript.

NEW JERSEY

HSPA

High School Proficiency Assessment in
Language Arts

HSPA – Language Arts
Independent
Study Schedule

INDEPENDENT STUDY SCHEDULE
NEW JERSEY HSPA IN LANGUAGE ARTS

The following study schedule will help you become thoroughly prepared for the HSPA in Language Arts. Although the schedule is designed as a six-week study program, if less time is available it can be condensed into three weeks by combining two weeks into one. If you are not enrolled in a structured course, be sure to set aside enough time—at least two hours each day—to study. Keep in mind that the more time you devote to studying for the HSPA in Language Arts, the more prepared and confident you will be on the day of the exam.

Week	Activity
1	Read the Passing the New Jersey HSPA section and familiarize yourself with the test format and procedures.
2	Read and study Chapter 1 (Review of Reading Skills), and complete all the problems. If you have particular trouble with any of the questions, review the relevant section again.
3	Read and study Chapter 2 (Review of Writing Skills), and complete all the problems. If you have particular trouble with any of the questions, review the relevant section again.
4	Read and study Chapter 3 (Review of Standard Written English), and complete all the problems. If you have particular trouble with any of the questions, review the relevant section again.
5	Take Practice Test 1, and after scoring your exam, carefully review the explanations to the questions you missed. If there are any types of questions that are particularly difficult for you, review those subjects by going over the appropriate section.
6	Take Practice Test 2, and after scoring your exam, carefully review the explanations to the questions you missed. If there are any types of questions that are particularly difficult for you, review those subjects by going over the appropriate section.

NEW JERSEY

HSPA

High School Proficiency Assessment in

Language Arts

Passing the New Jersey HSPA - Language Arts

PASSING THE NEW JERSEY HSPA IN LANGUAGE ARTS

ABOUT THIS BOOK

This book provides you with an accurate and complete representation of the New Jersey High School Proficiency Assessment (HSPA) in Language Arts. Inside you will find reviews that are designed to provide you with the information and strategies needed to do well on this section of the HSPA. We also provide two full-length practice tests, which are based on the official HSPA. REA's practice tests contain every type of question that you can expect to encounter on the Language Arts HSPA. Following each model test, you will find an answer key with detailed explanations designed to help you completely understand the test material. (*Note to educators*: Also included are over 100 class and homework problems that can be assigned to students. Answers to these questions can be found in the *HSPA Teacher's Guide*, which is available from REA.)

ABOUT THE TEST

Who takes the test and what is it used for?

The HSPA is mandatory for New Jersey high school juniors. It gauges students' knowledge and skills in the New Jersey Core Curriculum Content Standards. (The HSPA replaced the New Jersey High School Proficiency Test, or HSPT, in spring 2000.) Currently, the subjects tested are mathematics and language arts (other subjects may be given as field tests, but these are the only two on which students are graded).

New Jersey high school students are required to pass the entire test in order to graduate. Students who do not pass a section are given an opportunity to retake the test in the fall or spring of the 12th grade.

Who administers the test?

The HSPA was developed and is administered by the New Jersey State Department of Education and involves the assistance of educators throughout the state. The test development process is designed and implemented to ensure that the content and difficulty level of the test are appropriate.

When and where Is the test given?

The HSPA is administered in March and October. It is given at all New Jersey public high schools. The testing lasts for three days, and the HSPA may be taken on alternate days if a conflict—such as a religious obligation—exists.

To receive information on upcoming administrations of the HSPA, consult the Grade 11 High School Proficiency Assessment Parent Information Bulletin. The bulletin can be obtained from your guidance counselor or by contacting:

New Jersey State Department of Education
CN 500
Trenton, NJ 08265
Phone: (609) 292-4469
Website: www.state.nj.us/education

Is there a registration fee?

No. Because all New Jersey high school students are required to take this test, no fee is imposed.

HOW TO USE THIS BOOK

What do I study first?

Read over the reviews and the suggestions for test-taking. Studying the reviews thoroughly will reinforce the basic skills you will need to do well on the test. Be sure to take the practice tests to become familiar with the format and procedures involved with taking the actual HSPA.

To best utilize your study time, follow our HSPA Independent Study Schedule located in the front of this book. Brushing up on the areas you did well on wouldn't hurt either.

When should I start studying?

It is never too early to start studying for the HSPA. The earlier you begin, the more time you will have to sharpen your skills. Do not procrastinate! Cramming is *not* an effective way to study, since it does not allow you the time needed to learn the test material. The sooner you learn the format of the exam, the more time you will have to familiarize yourself with the exam content.

FORMAT OF THE HSPA LANGUAGE ARTS

Section	Time Alotted	Number of Questions
Writing: speculate (picture prompt)	30 minutes	1
Reading (narrative)	50 minutes	10 multiple-choice 2 open-ended
Writing (persuade)	60 minutes	1
Reading (persuasive)	45 minutes	10 multiple-choice 2 open-ended
Writing: (revise/edit)	25 minutes	1 assignment

As you can see, most of the questions on the HSPA are in multiple-choice format, with four options. There are exceptions: the Open-Ended Questions call for a written short answer of about one paragraph. Answer choices are not presented in the Open-Ended Questions. Furthermore, there are also two questions that call for essays to be written.

Language Arts Texts

There are two types of texts to which the student must respond:

- Narrative Text: A text that relates a story and asks questions that deal with characters, setting, theme, and climax.

- Persuasive Text: A text in which the writer attempts to convince the reader of his or her point of view.

Essay Prompts

There are also two prompts for which the student is expected to write an essay, and one for which the student is expected to revise an essay:

- **Writing:** *speculate (picture-linked prompt):* This task will ask the student to imagine, describe, and write a possible story behind a given picture.

- **Writing:** *persuade:* This task will ask the student to argue a side of a controversial issue.

- **Writing:** *revise/edit:* The student must correct errors that deal with capitalization, punctuation, and spelling, as well as clarity of expression.

ABOUT THE REVIEW SECTIONS

The reviews in this book are designed to help you sharpen the basic skills needed to approach the HSPA, as well as to provide strategies for attacking each type of question. You will also find exercises to reinforce what you have learned. By using the reviews in conjunction with the practice tests, you will put yourself in a position to master the HSPA.

Review of Reading Skills

In the Review of Reading Skills section you will find strategies for taking this portion of the test. Studying the information and completing the drills will improve your performance and help you pass the Language Arts section of the HSPA.

Review of Writing Skills

The Review of Writing Skills section provides strategies for the essay questions in the Language Arts section of the HSPA. Also included is review material that illustrates appropriate, unified, and focused essays, and gives tips on writing, editing, and polishing your essay.

Review of Standard Written English

The Review of Standard Written English section provides examples of the common mistakes people make in their use of written English. Learning how to avoid these mistakes will help make it possible for you to avoid losing points on the Language Arts essays and open-ended questions.

SCORING YOUR PRACTICE TESTS

The following information can be used in determining whether you have passed the practice tests provided in this book.

For each section there is a possible number of points that a student can receive. Each multiple-choice question equals 1 point and each open-ended question is worth 4 points. To determine points received, the student must add all correct responses for the multiple-choice, essay, and open-ended questions.

When determining open-ended points for the Language Arts sections, the number of points received is established by an evaluator. The score can range from 0 to 4. Each evaluator is specially trained for this type of test response. We advise that you have a teacher review and score all open-ended questions.

Determination of the essay scores is done in a different manner. The writing tasks are scored by professional readers. The scores for the Revising/Editing task are scored with the Revising/Editing Scoring Guide, a 0-4 point scale. All other writing samples are graded on the New Jersey Registered Holistic Scoring Rubric, a 0-6 point scale. Each writing sample is graded by two separate readers. Each reader is thoroughly trained to score these writing samples objectively. The two readers' scores for the Narrative task are averaged, and the two scores for the Persuasive task are added.

Once each section is graded, the total number of points received should be added together. This is your raw score.

Total Scaled Score

Your scores will be scaled to account for differences in various test administrations and forms; the scaled Language Arts score will be within a range of 100 to 300 points, with 200 being the minimum passing ("proficient") score. Since it is not possible to replicate the scaling formula for the HSPA, use the following standard to score your practice tests.

- **A passing (Proficient) score for the Language Arts test is a raw score of 29.5.**

Use the scoring worksheet below to score each of our two practice tests. While the score you earn on our practice tests should approximate the score you will receive on the HSPA, it should not be construed as a precise predictor of your actual test performance.

SCORING WORKSHEET

Writing (speculate)

_____   =   _____
points received   raw score
writing task

Reading (narrative)

_____   +   _____   =   _____
points received   points received   raw score
multiple-choice   open-ended

Writing (persuade)

_____   =   _____
points received   ×   2   raw score
writing task

Reading (persuasive)

_____   +   _____   =   _____
points received   points received   raw score
multiple-choice   open-ended

Writing (revise/edit)

(Note: At the time of this printing, this task was only being field-tested and not scored. Do not include this task in calculating your score on REA's practice tests. Check with your school district or with the Department of Education to determine if it will be graded in upcoming administrations.)

TEST-TAKING TIPS

Although you may not be familiar with standardized tests such as the HSPA, there are many ways to acquaint yourself with this type of examination and help alleviate your test-taking anxieties. Listed below are ways to help you become accustomed to the HSPA, some of which may be applied to other standardized tests as well.

Become comfortable with the format of the HSPA. When you are practicing, simulate the conditions under which you will be taking the actual test. Stay calm and pace yourself. After simulating the test only a couple of times, you will boost your chances of doing well, and you will be able to sit for the actual HSPA with greater confidence.

Read all of the possible answers. Just because you think you have found the correct response, do not automatically assume that it is the best answer. Read through each choice to be sure that you are not making a mistake by jumping to conclusions.

Use the process of elimination. Go through each possible response to a question and eliminate as many of the answer choices as possible. By eliminating two answer choices, you can vastly improve your chances of getting the item correct, since there will only be two choices left from which to make your guess.

Work quickly and steadily. You will have only minutes to work on each section, so work quickly and steadily to avoid getting waylaid by any one problem. Taking the practice tests in this book will help you learn to budget your precious time.

Learn the directions and format for each section of the test. Familiarizing yourself with the directions and format of the different test sections will not only save time, but will also help you avoid anxiety (and the mistakes caused by getting anxious).

Work on the easier questions first. If you find yourself working too long on one question, flag it in your test booklet and continue. After you have answered all of the questions that you can, go back to the ones you have skipped.

Be sure that the answer oval you are marking corresponds to the number of the question in the test booklet. Since the multiple-choice sections are graded by machine, marking one wrong answer can throw off your answer key and your score. Be extremely careful.

Eliminate obvious wrong answers. Sometimes an HSPA question will have one or two answer choices that are a little odd. These answers will be obviously wrong for one of several reasons: they may be impossible given the conditions of the problem, they may violate mathematical rules or principles, or they may be illogical. Being able to spot obvious wrong answers before you finish a problem gives you an advantage because you will be able to make a more educated guess from the remaining choices even if you are unable to fully solve the problem.

Work from answer choices. One of the ways you can use a multiple-choice format to your advantage is to work backwards from the answer choices to solve a problem. This is not a strategy you can use all the time, but it can be helpful if you can just plug the choices into a given statement or equation. The answer choices can often narrow the scope of responses. You may be able to make an educated guess based on eliminating choices that you know do not fit into the problem.

THE DAY OF THE TEST

Before the Test

On the day of the test, you should wake up early (it is hoped after a decent night's rest) and have a good breakfast. Make sure to dress comfortably, so that you are not distracted by being too hot or too cold while taking the test. Also, plan to arrive at the test center early. This will allow you to collect your thoughts and relax before the test, and will also spare you the anguish that comes with being late. As an added incentive to make sure you arrive early, keep in mind that *no one* will be allowed into the test session after the test has begun.

If you would like, you may wear a watch to the test center. However, you may not wear one that makes noise, because it may disturb the other test-takers. No dictionaries, textbooks, notebooks, briefcases, or packages will be permitted; drinking, smoking, and eating are prohibited. You will be given a "Writer's Checklist" to help you present your ideas effectively as you write and/or edit, and pencils will be provided for your use.

During the Test

Once you enter the test center, follow all of the rules and instructions given by the test supervisor. If you do not, you risk being dismissed from the test and having your HSPA scores canceled.

When all of the test materials have been passed out, the test supervisor will give you directions for filling out your answer sheet. You must fill out this sheet carefully since this information will be printed on your score report. Fill out your name exactly as it appears on your identification documents, unless otherwise instructed.

You will be provided with pages designated for prewriting for some tasks, but all answers and finished essays must be marked in the answer folder. Mark your answers in the appropriate spaces in the answer folder. Each numbered row will contain four ovals corresponding to each answer choice for that question. Fill in the oval that corresponds to your answer darkly, completely, and neatly. You can change your answer, but be sure to completely erase your old answer. Only one answer should be marked. This is very important, as your answer sheet will be machine-scored and stray lines or unnecessary marks may cause the machine to score your answers incorrectly.

After the Test

Once your test materials have been collected, you will be dismissed. Go home and relax—you deserve it! Your score report will arrive in about five weeks.

NEW JERSEY

HSPA

High School Proficiency Assessment in

Language Arts

CHAPTER 1

Review of Reading
Skills

REVIEW OF READING SKILLS

I.   **Strategies for the Language Arts Section**
II. **Reading Narrative Text**
III. **Reading Persuasive Text**

This review is designed to prepare you for the Language Arts section of the New Jersey High School Proficiency Assessment. The review contains information about the types of passages you will be asked to read and the kinds of questions you will be expected to answer. You will also find tips and strategies to help you answer the questions quickly and accurately. Studying this review, together with taking the two practice tests in this book, will help you develop the skills you need to perform well on the Language Arts section of the HSPA.

Types of Passages

The Language Arts section of the HSPA requires the student to interpret two types of text: narrative and persuasive. Since these types differ in content and require specialized reading skills and approaches, this review provides a section on each type, along with passages, sample questions, and detailed explanations on how to read and answer these practice questions.

Types of Questions

Each section of text in the Language Arts section of the HSPA will be followed by 12 questions. The total number of Language Arts questions is 24. With each type of passage, you will be asked to answer multiple-choice Language Arts questions that require you to have read and fully understood the text.

A smaller group of questions gauges your ability to discuss in writing the issues raised and implied by a text. Open-ended questions require you to read *between the lines,* working at an inferential level and making connections between the ideas within the text and relevant ideas outside of the literal text.

Open-ended questions are scored using a point scale running from 0-4.

These levels reflect varying degrees of accuracy and completeness. The evaluation of open-ended responses focuses on your thinking ability and your demonstration of a particular level of reading comprehension. A score point of 0 means the response is irrelevant or off-topic. A score point of 1 means the response demonstrates minimal understanding of the task, does not complete the requirements, and uses the text very little or not at all. A score point of 2 means the response may correspond with all the requirements, but with only partial understanding and uses text incorrectly or unsuccessfully, with an inconsistent or flawed explanation. A score point of 3 means the response demonstrates an understanding of the text and completes all requirements while presenting the writer's conclusions or opinions, using examples from the text for support. A grade of 4 demonstrates a clear understanding of the text, completes all requirements, and provides an especially insightful explanation or opinion that builds off of the text. You will find many samples of successful and unsuccessful responses in this book to help you prepare for the open-ended questions.

I. Strategies for the Language Arts Section

Before the test, you should use this plan:

1. Study this review section to learn about the kinds of text and questions to expect.

2. Do the practice questions in this review section as well as the two practice tests in this test prep. After you have answered the questions, carefully read the explanations of the answers, even if you answered correctly. The more you know about how the questions and answers work, the better you will do on the Language Arts section.

When reading the text and answering the questions, keep these strategies for effective reading in mind:

1. Preview: Your first step should be to look over the text and questions quickly to see what the text contains and what the questions ask. Take about 30 seconds to preview the material. At this point, do not spend time reading all of the answer choices.

2. Active reading: After you preview, read the text carefully and actively. Keep in mind the questions you previewed and mark important words or sections of the text. Consult sections II through III of this review to learn what to look for in each of the types of text.

3. Answer the questions: Once you have read the text actively, you are ready to answer the questions. Remember that while some answers can be found in the text on a literal level, you also need to work at an inferential level and to think about how the text can apply to situations or ideas outside of the text itself.

4. Review the text: As you answer the questions, look back at the text when necessary to help you eliminate incorrect answers and determine the correct answer. This process of working back and forth between the questions and the text helps you to answer with speed and accuracy.

Additional Reading Tips

➤ Do not hesitate to write on the text as you read. Underlining key words or names, bracketing important sentences, and circling transitional words ("however," "but," "yet," "on the other hand," "although," etc.) will help you to locate what you need to answer the questions. At the same time, do not mark too much of the text, as this extra work might slow you down.

➤ When a question asks you to draw inferences, the correct answer will reflect what is implied in the passage, rather than what is directly stated.

➤ Focus on one question at a time.

➤ Eliminate wrong answers, decide on your response, and move on to the next question. Do not waste time fretting about a difficult question. If you cannot get an answer after two attempts, answer as best as you can and focus your energy on the next question. Sometimes you will discover or think of the answer to a previous question in the course of answering another question.

➤ Pay careful attention to the wording of each question. You may be asked to select the BEST or MOST LIKELY answer. Or you may be asked to decide which answer is NOT consistent with the text. Noticing these key words will affect your ability to choose the correct answer.

II. Reading Narrative Text

The narrative text in the HSPA constitutes works of *fiction* between 2,100 and 3,300 words in length, written for the purpose of telling a story.

Most HSPA narratives are realistic fiction, with characters, settings, and events that are probable and reflect ordinary people's lives in everyday situations. Realistic fiction writers include Judy Blume, S.E. Hinton, Bobbie Ann Mason, and Cynthia Rylant. You will need to be aware of the distinction between realistic fiction and other types of fiction, like fantasy/science fiction and historical fiction. Fantasy stories take place in imaginary settings, and science fiction explores futuristic worlds that might be created by scientific and technological developments. J.R.R. Tolkien's *The Hobbit* is a fantasy narrative; H.G. Wells' *The Time Machine* and Ray Bradbury's *Fahrenheit 451* are examples of science fiction. Historical fiction situates a story in relation to historical events or figures, like Charles Dickens' *A Tale of Two Cities*, a novel set during the French Revolution. While it is useful to recognize the differences between these and other genres of fiction, for the HSPA you need to be most familiar with realistic stories.

When reading a narrative text, you will need to answer questions that ask you to do the following:

- Determine a story's point of view or a change in point of view. A story might first tell you what one character is thinking or feeling and then introduce another character's perspective. In addition to the view from which a story is told, point of view can also refer to a character's attitude toward an event, setting, or another person.

- Infer the meaning of a phrase that uses figurative language such as a simile or a metaphor. A simile presents a comparison between two things using the word "like" or "as"; a metaphor asserts that one thing is another thing. For example, a story might describe a girl to be "moving down the path like an injured bird." You would choose the answer that best expresses the meaning of this simile: "She was limping."

- Select the best definition for a word based on its use in the narrative.

- Select a word or words that best describe a character. Descriptive adjectives for characters include bold, shy, charming, sincere, reserved, honest, and confident.

- Choose a word that characterizes the author's tone. Possible styles include comic, philosophical, sarcastic, uplifting, depressing, or matter-of-fact.

- Identify the story's prominent theme or themes, such as parent/child conflicts, dealing with loss, the meaning of responsibility, learning from mistakes, or confronting fear.

- Recognize the turning point and key events in the narrative. A story's turning point is a moment, realization, or incident in which a significant change occurs. That change might result in a character's decision or a resolution to the problem presented in the story.

- Demonstrate your knowledge about reading. For narrative text, this type of question includes choosing the best strategy to use in answering another question on the text, deciding which life experience would help you to understand the story, and determining the reason why an author uses particular conventions like italics, quotation marks, or parentheses.

Exercise 1: Narrative Passage

> **DIRECTIONS**: The following excerpt presents the first two paragraphs of a story entitled "Repairs." You may make notes and underline as you read and answer the questions that follow.

"Repairs"

Sam was not always so quiet at school. With his gifts of wit and a certain wisdom beyond his age, he had once been, if not the center of attention, at least an active part of the periphery. Sarah remembered when Sam, her younger sibling by a year and a half, had charmed teachers and students alike with his fanciful tales: clumsy sailors who save the ship from disaster, crooked politicians made straight by bands of enraged high school sophomores, rock stars-turned-ostrich farmers trying to live simpler, less prominent lives.

But Sarah could not recall Sam telling one of his stories for several months. When asked, he would shrug, say something about not forcing the fickle muse, and slip off by himself at the earliest possible moment. In fact, since their friend Charlie had died last July, Sam had withdrawn, his spirit shriveled somehow like a tire with a slow but steady leak. Their parents, who noticed but avoided discussing changes in their children's emotions and behavior, had figured, wrongly, that time would fix what they could not.

1. How does Sarah know that Sam has changed?

    (A) He wants to be the center of attention.

    (B) He looks drawn and tired.

    (C) He talks about the friend he lost.

    (D) He no longer tells his inventive stories.

2. Based on this story's first two paragraphs, how would the parents MOST LIKELY react if Sarah started to show signs of depression?

    (A) They would not ask her what was wrong.

    (B) They would take her to a counselor.

    (C) They would tell her that they were willing to listen when she was ready to talk.

    (D) They would ask Sam what was wrong with his sister.

3. The end of the first paragraph reads: ". . .rock stars-turned-ostrich farmers trying to live simpler, less *prominent* lives." Which word means the OPPOSITE of *prominent*?

    (A) Visible   (C) Famous

    (B) Unknown   (D) Unappreciated

4. Given the story's title, "Repairs," what would you expect to happen in a positive ending to the story?

    (A) Sam remains withdrawn.

    (B) The characters learn how to fix a flat tire.

    (C) The parents help Sam to recover from the loss of his friend.

    (D) The parents and children fail to mend their split family.

5. Which detail would be the LEAST IMPORTANT to include if you were retelling this story to a friend?

    (A) Sarah and Sam's friend died last July.

    (B) Sam has become quiet and reclusive.

    (C) Sarah is a year and a half older than Sam.

    (D) Sam has a reputation as a storyteller.

DIRECTIONS FOR QUESTION 6: Write your answer in the space provided, referring to the excerpt from the story "Repairs." Be sure to address all parts of the question.

---

6.   Discuss TWO reasons why the title "Repairs" is appropriate for this story.

   •   What does the title imply about the characters?

   •   Use details from the excerpt to explain and support your discussion.

In approaching this practice narrative, you should first *preview the paragraphs and the questions.* You might skim the paragraphs and then read the questions (but not necessarily the answer choices) to find out what you need to look for upon a careful reading.

Next, you should *read actively,* getting a sense of who the characters are: Sam before and after his change, Sarah, Charlie, the parents. Underline or mark important words, phrases, or literary devices. Note, for instance, the simile in paragraph two comparing Sam's spirit to a slowly deflating tire. To *answer the questions,* read the question and the four answer choices carefully and *look back* at the passage to help you narrow your choice.

III. Reading Persuasive Text

The persuasive text combines fact and opinion with the purpose of persuading readers to share (or at least to understand) a certain point of view. This type of text openly advocates a particular stand on an issue or an approach to a problem. By presenting a point of view and providing factual and/or anecdotal evidence, a writer aims to support his/her argument. When reading persuasive texts, be aware that writers may draw upon not only facts but also beliefs, value judgments, and opinions. Writers might exaggerate, present convincing statistics, offer powerful examples, and employ emotionally charged words to make their argument. You will need to understand what the writer says and to recognize how and why a writer uses language to influence readers' opinions and thinking. Persuasive texts on the HSPA may be excerpted or used in full and will range from 1000 to 1600 words.

To familiarize yourself with this kind of reading, you should read the editorial sections of your local newspaper, looking both at the op-eds and the letters to the editor. Other persuasive text includes speeches, essays, book and movie reviews, charitable campaign appeals, debates, magazine editorials, and political literature.

When reading a persuasive text, you will need to answer questions that ask you to do the following:

- Decide which statement best expresses the main point of the text or a section of the text.

- Distinguish between fact and opinion. Whereas a statement such as "78 percent of high school teachers oppose book censorship" could be a fact based on a particular survey, a statement like "Book censorship damages our intellectual freedom" is an opinion. With persuasive text, you need to evaluate the kind of evidence provided.

- Decide which statement best supports or undermines a writer's argument.

- Identify instances of exaggeration, emotional appeal, or other methods of persuasion in the text.

- Compare the perspectives of two different writers. After reading two editorials with opposing views on an issue, you might then be asked "with which of the following statements would both authors most likely agree?"

Exercise 2: Persuasive Text

DIRECTIONS: Please read the following essay and answer the questions that follow.

Adapted from: "Religion Without Dogma"
by C.S. Lewis

Professor Hostead, in his article "Modern Agnosticism Justified," argues that a) religion is basically belief in God and immortality, b) most religions consist of "*accretions of dogma and mythology*" that science has disproven, c) it would be desirable, if it were possible, to keep the basic religious belief without those accumulations of religious notions and legends, but that d) science has rendered even the basic elements of religion almost as incredible as the "accretions." For the doctrine of immortality involves the view that man is a composite creature, a soul in a state of symbiosis with a physical organism. But science can successfully regard man only monastically, as a single organism whose psychological characteristics all arise from his physical nature; the soul then becomes indefensible. In conclusion, Professor Hostead asserts that our only hope rests in empirical, observable evidence for the existence of the soul; in fact, in the findings of psychical research.

My disagreement with Professor Hostead starts at the beginning. I do not consider the essence of religion as simply the belief in God and immortality. Early Judaism, for example, didn't accept immortality. The human soul in Sheol (the afterworld) took no account of Jehovah, and God in turn took no account of the soul. In Sheol all things are forgotten. The religion revolved around the ritual and ethical demands of God and on the blessings people received from him. During earthly life these blessings were usually material in nature: happy life, many children, good health, and such. But we do see a more religious note also. The Jew hungers for the living God; he obeys God's laws devoutly; he considers himself as impure and sinful in Jehovah's presence. God is the sole object of worship. Buddhism makes the doctrine of immortality vital, while we find little in the way of that which is religious. The existence of the gods is not denied, but it has no religious significance. In Stoicism, again, both the practice of religion and the belief in immortality are variables, not absolute traits of religion. Even within Christianity itself we find, as in Stoicism, the subordinate position of immortality.

1. Which of the following best defines the phrase *"accretions of dogma and mythology"* as it is used in the first paragraph?

   (A) Combinations of fact and fiction

   (B) Conflicts of sound principles and unsound theories

   (C) Implications and ideas of religion

   (D) Religious ideas and fables that have gradually accumulated to form accepted religious belief

2. What is the main idea of the entire passage?

   (A) Belief in God is scientifically valid.

   (B) Professor Hostead's assumption that the essence of religion is the belief in God and immortality is incorrect.

   (C) Neither Judaism, Buddhism, Stoicism, nor Christianity fit into Hostead's definition of religion.

(D) Judaism, Buddhism, Stoicism, and Christianity are all valid ideologies in their regard for immortality and belief in God.

3. The writer's purpose in this passage is to

(A) outline basic tenets of Judaism, Buddhism, Stoicism, and Christianity.

(B) establish scientific credibility of four ideologies so as to undermine Hostead's positions.

(C) attack Hostead's views by establishing the vulnerability of Hostead's first position.

(D) define the essence of religion.

4. The writer uses Judaism, Buddhism, Stoicism, and Christianity to illustrate

(A) the superiority of Christianity over the other three religions.

(B) that the essence of religion is not necessarily belief in God and immortality.

(C) empirical evidence for the soul, the psychical research, which Hostead requires as proof for the soul.

(D) the validity of religious thought over a scientific system devoid of religious, spiritual beliefs.

5. Which of the following lists of topics best organizes the information in this passage?

(A) I. Hostead's definition of religion

II. Writer's definition of religion

III. Illustrations to support a new definition

(B) I. Hostead's definition of religion

II. Writer's definition of Judaism

III. Writer's comparison of other ideologies to Judaism

(C) I. Hostead's position regarding religion

II. Writer's problem with Hostead's position

III. Illustrations to support objections

(D) I. Hostead's definition of religion

II. Hostead's definition of science

III. Writer's position against Hostead's definition of religion and science

6. How does the example of Judaism prove an error in Hostead's assertions?

    •   Support your response by referring to the text.

In approaching this practice persuasive passage, you should first *preview the paragraphs and the questions.* You might skim the paragraphs and then read the questions (but not necessarily the answer choices) to find out what you need to look for upon a careful reading.

Next, you should *read actively,* getting a sense of what the writer's argument is and why he is making it. To *answer the questions,* read the question and the four answer choices carefully and *look back* at the passage to help you narrow your choice.

READING SKILLS EXERCISES

ANSWER KEY

Exercise 1 – Narrative Passage

1. (D)	2. (A)	3. (B)
4. (C)	5. (C)	6. see sample responses

Exercise 2 – Persuasive Text

1. (D)	2. (B)	3. (C)
4. (B)	5. (C)	6. see sample responses

DETAILED EXPLANATIONS
OF ANSWERS

Exercise 1: Narrative Passage

1. **(D)** Since Sarah notices that Sam does not tell stories like he did before (D) is correct. This question asks you to look at what the story says on a literal level. We read that Sam has not told a story for months, but we do not read that (A) he wants to be the center of attention, (B) he looks drawn and tired, or (C) he talks about the friend that died. The mention of the "center of attention" in paragraph one and the statement that "Sam had withdrawn" in paragraph two might mislead you to choose (A) or (C), so you need to read carefully what the question asks and how the answer choices are worded.

2. **(A)** This question requires that you take what is said about the parents and apply that information to a hypothetical situation. Since the parents avoid discussing their children's behavior, you can predict that (A) they would not ask Sarah what was wrong. Their hands-off approach to parenting makes it unlikely that they would (B) take her to a counselor, (C) tell her they were willing to listen, or (D) ask Sam about his sister. Again, in this type of question you are using details in the narrative to consider a situation outside of the narrative itself.

3. **(B)** This question is a definitional question, asking you to determine the meaning of "prominent" in the context of the sentence. You need to find the word that means the opposite of prominent. Once you determine that prominent people are, like rock stars, (A) visible and (C) famous, you know that these two choices are incorrect since they mean the same as prominent. In choosing between (B) unknown and (D) unappreciated, unknown is more closely the opposite of prominent. To be appreciated and to be prominent are not necessarily the same.

4. **(C)** This question asks you to read *beyond* the lines of the paragraphs you have read to imagine an ending to the story that takes into account the story's title. A positive reading of the word "Repairs" makes (A) and (D) incorrect. An ending in which (A) Sam remains withdrawn or (D) the family fails to mend itself would not fulfill the change implied in repairing something for the better. (B) is incorrect; this possible ending takes the simile of Sam's spirit as a leaky tire too literally. Thus, an ending

in which (C) the parents help Sam to recover from the loss of his friend reflects the meaning of "Repairs."

5. **(C)** This question gauges your knowledge of reading by asking you to think about the relative importance of details in the story. That Sam (D) has a reputation as a storyteller, but has (B) become quiet and reclusive are central to an understanding of the story. That (A) Sarah and Sam's friend died is the crucial component in understanding the change in Sam's personality. But the difference in age between sister and brother is a supporting, not an essential, detail if you were to retell the story. Thus, (C) Sarah is a year and a half older than Sam is the correct answer.

6. Here are two sample responses to this open-ended question, representing both "good" and "poor" responses. Notice that the good response (representing a score of 3 or 4) explains TWO reasons for the title's appropriateness, showing how the title relates to the characters and using ample evidence from the story for support. The poor response (representing a score of 2 or 1) gives ONE reason, with minimal support from the story that shows a literal reading of the text.

GOOD RESPONSE

As the title "Repairs" indicates, the lives of the characters are in need of mending. First, Sam's happiness needs repairing, since he is mourning the loss of his friend. The visible signs of Sam's broken state are his isolation and his lack of desire to tell stories. His sister Sarah knows that Sam has changed for the worse. Also, Sam's spirit is compared to a flat tire. Second, the relationship between Sam and his parents needs mending. The parents are aware of their son's grief but are not getting involved. They need to help their son heal. Then, maybe the relationship between the parents and the children can heal, too. If the parents can help "fix" Sam's depression, the story will live up to its title. The title suits the characters' lives and sets up the expectation that the troubles will get better.

POOR RESPONSE

One reason is that Sam seems "like a tire with a slow but steady leak." So he needs repairs. He is also too quiet and has to tell his stories again. He used to tell stories at school about sailors, politicians, and ostrich farmers. The title clearly reflects Sam's life, so the title is appropriate.

Exercise 2: Persuasive Text

1. **(D)**   Item (c) in the first paragraph refers to this term with a correct definition: "those accumulations of religious notions and legends." (A) is incorrect; the first paragraph doesn't suggest that these "accretions" are anything but "incredible" and fiction. (B) is incorrect; the first paragraph maintains that Hostead's position rejects any soundness in such accretions. (C) is incorrect; again, "accretions," according to contextual clues, doesn't mean "implications," but rather "accumulations."

2. **(B)**   Hostead's first assumption makes that statement about the essence of religion while the second sentence in paragraph two disputes it. (A) is incorrect; paragraph one defines Hostead's position, while the second paragraph addresses the first position, which doesn't deal with scientific validity of any belief in God. (C) is incorrect; these four ideologies are simply used to illustrate that immortality is not necessarily the essence of a religion, but the central idea of the passage is not the defense of these ideologies. (D) is incorrect; the writer is not defending the validity of those ideologies, but using them to attack one of Hostead's points.

3. **(C)**   The first two sentences of the second paragraph state this purpose exactly. (A) is incorrect; the writer only touches on one aspect of each of these beliefs to disprove Hostead's first point. (B) is incorrect; the writer touches on only the first position, which does not deal with scientific credibility. (D) is incorrect; the writer disputes Hostead's definition of essence of religion rather than provide his own definition.

4. **(B)**   The writer states this in the second sentence of the second paragraph, and proceeds to illustrate his point with those four beliefs. (A) is incorrect; the writer makes no statement or inference of that nature; he treats the four equally. (C) is incorrect; the writer doesn't address a psychical approach. (D) is incorrect; the writer is not testifying to the validity of any of these ideologies, but using them to illustrate the error of Hostead's first contention.

5. **(C)**   Paragraph one itemizes Hostead's positions and a conclusion while paragraph two begins with the writer's objection to Hostead's position followed by illustrations from four main streams of religious thought. (A) is incorrect; neither Hostead nor the writer defines religion. (B) is incorrect; Hostead doesn't define religion; the writer neither defines Judaism nor uses it as a basis of comparison. (D) is incorrect; again, Hostead defines neither religion nor science while the writer never addresses science.

6. Here are two sample responses to this open-ended question, representing both "good" and "poor" responses. Notice that the good response (representing a score of 3 or 4) explains in an appropriately complex way how Judaism is used to disprove Hostead's assertion. The poor response (representing a score of 2 or 1) gives an oversimplified response, with minimal support from the passage.

GOOD RESPONSE

Professor Hostead says in his first assertion that religion is basically belief in God and immortality. However, C.S. Lewis' essay disproves that assertion in a way that calls into question the accuracy of Hostead's thinking. Judaism is shown to not have an intrinsic belief in immortality, yet still be a religion.

Lewis mentions that early Judaism "didn't accept immortality." Though Sheol (the afterworld) was part of the system of belief, it was considered to be apart from God, a place where "all things are forgotten." Yet, despite this, Judaism was nonetheless very much a religion. Its practitioners hungered for the living God, and made their deity the focus of their lives.

By showing that Judaism was not basically a "belief in God and immortality," yet was a religion nonetheless, the passage disproves Professor Hostead's first assertion.

POOR RESPONSE

The professor says that what religion is, is belief in God and immortality. However, the passage shows this can't be true, because the religion of Judaism has God but doesn't really have immortality. So the professor is proved wrong, because what he said does not stand up to the example.

Now that you have studied this Review of Reading Skills section, you are ready to move on to the Review of Writing Skills in the next chapter.

NEW JERSEY

HSPA

High School Proficiency Assessment in

Language Arts

CHAPTER 2

Review of Writing Skills

REVIEW OF WRITING SKILLS

Why Essays Exist

People write essays for purposes other than testing. Some of our best thinkers have written essays, which we continue to read from generation to generation. Essays offer the reader a logical, coherent, and imaginative written composition, showing the nature or consequences of a single controlling idea when considered from the writer's unique point of view. Writers use essays to communicate their opinion or position on a topic to readers who cannot be present during their live conversation. Writers use essays to help readers understand or learn about something that readers should or might want to know or do. Essays always express more or less directly the author's opinion, belief, position, or knowledge (backed by evidence) about the idea or object in question.

Organization

For this test you will need to recognize and generate the elements of an "excellent" essay. In essence, you will be taking the principles covered in Part I of this review and utilizing them to create your own original essay. You will need to do so to succeed on the persuasive writing task and also in answering the open-ended questions from the reading assignments. With that in mind, read carefully the standards and explanations below to prepare you for what to look for in your own essay response.

Essay Writing

In academic writing, two purposes dominate essays:

1. Persuasion through argumentation using one, some, or all of the logical patterns described below, and/or

2. Informing and educating through analysis and using one, some, or all of the logical patterns described below.

All of an essay's organizational strategies may be used to argue in writing. The author offers reasons and/or evidence so an audience will be inclined to believe the position that the author presents about the idea under discussion. Writers use seven basic strategies to organize information and ideas in essays to help prove their point (thesis). All of these strategies might be useful in arguing for an idea and persuading a reader to see the issue the writer's way. Your job is to use strategies that are appropriate to demonstrate your thesis. For example, you may wish to use comparison/contrast to demonstrate that one thing or idea is better or worse than another.

Seven Steps to Prove a Thesis

1. Show how a *process* or procedure does or should work step by step in time.

2. *Compare or contrast* two or more things or ideas to show important differences or similarities.

3. *Identify a problem* and then explain how to solve it.

4. *Analyze* into its components, or *classify* by its types or categories, an idea or thing to show how it is put together, how it works, or how it is designed.

5. *Explain* why something happens to produce a particular result or set of results.

6. *Describe* the particular individual characteristics, beauty, and features of a place, person(s), time, or idea.

7. *Define* what a thing is or what an idea means.

Depending upon the purpose of the essay, one pattern tends to dominate the discussion question. (For example, the writer might use *description* and *explanation* to define the varied meanings of "love.")

The Writing Process: Controlling Organization, Paragraph Development, Sentence Structure, Usage, and Mechanical Conventions

During this test you will be called upon to exercise control over your writing by using the writing process and by knowing the pitfalls of weak writing and correcting them. Using the steps outlined below, compose your essay in the order suggested and note the elements and qualities to correct during each stage of the process of composing your essay test response. Make your corrections during the appropriate stage of the writing process; to correct errors at the wrong stage may waste time and interfere with your producing the best essay response.

Composing Your Essay: Using the Writing Process

Most of us think—erroneously—that writers just sit down and churn out a wonderful essay or story in one sitting in a flash of genius and inspiration. This is not true. Writers use the writing process from start to finish to help them write a clear document. If you do not reflect on your composition in stages and make changes as you develop it, you will not recognize all the problems or errors in it. Don't try to write an essay in one draft and leave the room. Stay and look through it. Reflect upon it using the writing process in the following way.

The writing process has five basic steps: (1) Prewriting or Planning time, (2) Rough Drafting, (3) Organizing and Revising the ideas (not the words or sentences themselves), (4) Polishing or Editing (making sure sentences themselves are sentences, that the words you use are the right words, and that the spelling and punctuation are correct), and (5) Proof-reading to make sure no little mistakes are left.

Using this process does not mean that you have to write five drafts. Write *one* draft (stages 1 and 2), leaving space for corrections (e.g., writing on every other line); then, work on the existing draft through the rest of the stages (3 through 5). If time allows, you may want to do the whole process on scrap paper and then copy the finished product onto the allotted test paper. But if you do copy it, make sure you proofread your copy once more, looking for errors that may have crept in during the transcribing process.

For example, assume you have 60 minutes for your essay. You might allocate your time for the five writing steps in this manner:

1. Prewriting, Planning: 5 minutes

2. Rough Drafting: 20 minutes

3. Organizing, checking evidence, checking "flow," and paragraphing: 25 minutes

4. Polishing, Editing: 5–10 minutes

5. Proofreading: 2–5 minutes

If you have more time or less time, adjust this schedule proportionately. Practice this with someone timing you.

Writing Your Essay

Prewriting/Planning Time

Read the essay question and decide on your purpose. Do you want to persuade your reader? Or are you setting out to explain something?

Sample: "Television is bad for people."

Do you agree or disagree with this statement? Decide. Take a stand. Don't be noncommittal. Write down the statement of your position.

Sample: I agree that television is bad for people.

or

Television is an excellent learning tool and is good for most people.

This is your thesis.

Considering Your Audience

The writer's responsibility is to write clearly, honestly, and cleanly for the reader's sake. Essays would be pointless without an audience. Why write an essay if no one wants or needs to read it? Why add evidence, organize your ideas, or correct bad grammar? The reason to do any of these things is that someone out there needs to understand what you mean or say. What would the audience need to know in order to believe you or to come over to your position? Imagine someone you know (visualize her — name him) listening to you declare your position or opinion and then saying, "Oh yeah? Prove it!"

In writing your essay, make sure to answer the following questions:

What evidence do you need to prove your idea to this skeptic?

What would s/he disagree with you about?

What does s/he share with you as common knowledge?

What does s/he need to be told by you?

Controlling Your Point of View

We may write essays from one of three points of view, depending upon the essay's audience. The points of view below are discussed from informal to formal.

1. Subjective/Personal Point of View:

    "I think . . .

    "I feel . . .

    "I believe . . . cars are more trouble than they are worth."

2. Second Person (We . . . You; I . . . You): "If *you* own a car, *you* soon find out that it is more trouble than it is worth."

3. Third Person Point of View (focuses on the idea, not what "I" think of it): "*Cars* are more trouble than *they* are worth."

Stick with one or another; don't switch your "point of view" in the middle. Any one is acceptable.

Considering Your Support

Next, during prewriting, jot down a few phrases that show ideas and examples that support your point of view. Do this quickly on a separate piece of paper for about *five minutes*. Don't try to outline, simply *list things* that you think might be important to discuss. After you have listed several, pick at least three to five things you want or need to discuss, and number them in the order of importance that is relevant to proving your point.

Writing Your Rough Draft

Spend about *20 minutes* writing your *rough draft* (for the extended writing assignments, pages will be provided for this purpose). Looking over at your prewriting list, write down what you think is useful to prove your point in the order you think best to convince the reader. Be sure to *use real evidence* from your life experience or knowledge to support what you say. You do not have to draw evidence from books; your own life is equally appropriate.

For example, don't write, "Cars are more trouble to fix than bicycles" and then not show evidence for your idea. Give *examples* of what you mean: "*For example*, my father's Buick needs 200 parts to make one brake work, but my bicycle only has four pieces that make up the brakes, and I can replace those myself." Write naturally and quickly. Don't worry too much at this point about paragraphing, spelling, punctuation — just write down what you think or want to say in the order determined on your list.

Transitions

To help the reader follow the flow of your ideas, and to help unify the essay, use transitions to show the connections among your ideas. You may use transitions either at the beginnings of paragraphs, or you may use them to show the connections among ideas within a single paragraph.

Here are some typical transitional words and phrases that you should use when writing your essay.

To link similar ideas, use the words:

again	for example	likewise
also	for instance	moreover
and	further	nor
another	furthermore	of course
besides	in addition	similarly
equally important	in like manner	too

To link dissimilar/contradictory ideas, use words such as:

although	however	otherwise
and yet	in spite of	provided that
as if	instead	still
but	nevertheless	yet
conversely	on the contrary	
even if	on the other hand	

To indicate cause, purpose, or result, use:

as	for	so
as a result	for this reason	then
because	hence	therefore
consequently	since	thus

To indicate time or position, use words like:

above	before	meanwhile
across	beyond	next
afterward	eventually	presently

around	finally	second
at once	first	thereafter
at the present time	here	thereupon

To indicate an example or summary, use phrases such as:

as a result	in any event	in short
as I have said	in brief	on the whole
for example	in conclusion	to sum up
for instance	in fact	
in any case	in other words	

Grammar

Correct use of grammar is also a very important element in writing a good essay. Therefore, you should make sure to correctly employ all of the rules of standard written English. Be sure to see the Review of Standard Written English in the following chapter.

Providing Evidence in Your Essay

You may employ any one of the seven steps previously listed to prove any thesis that you maintain is true. You may call on evidence from one or all of the four following types to support the thesis of your essay. Identify which type(s) of evidence you can use to prove the points of your essay. In test situations, most essayists use anecdotal evidence or analogy to explain, describe, or prove a thesis. But if you know salient facts or statistics, don't hesitate to call upon them.

1. **Hard data (facts, statistics, scientific evidence, research)** — documented evidence that has been verified to be true.

2. **Expert opinions** — assertions, usually by authorities on the matter under discussion.

3. **Anecdotal evidence** — stories from the writer's own experience and knowledge that illustrate a particular point or idea.

4. **Analogies** — show a resemblance between one phenomenon and another.

Organizing and Reviewing the Paragraphs

The unit of work for revising is the paragraph. After you have written what you wanted to say based on your prewriting list, spend about *25 minutes* revising your draft by looking to see if you need to indent for paragraphs anywhere. If you do, make a little proofreader's mark (¶) to indicate to the reader that you think a paragraph should start here. Check to see if you want to add anything that would make your opinion more convincing. Be sure to supply useful transitions to keep up the flow and maintain the focus of your ideas. If you don't have room on the paper, or if your new paragraph shows up out of order, add that paragraph and indicate with a number or some other mark where you want it to go. Check to *make sure* that you gave examples or illustrations for your statements. In the examples below, two paragraphs are offered: one without concrete evidence and one with evidence for its idea. Study each. Note the topic sentence (**T**) and how that sentence is or is not supported with evidence.

Paragraphing With and Without Evidence

(**T**) Television is bad for people. *Watching television takes time away from other things.* Programs on television are often stupid and depict crimes that people later copy. Television takes time away from loved ones, and it often becomes addictive. So, television is bad for people because it is no good.

Comment: In this example, the author has not given any concrete evidence for any of the good ideas presented. S/he just declares them to be so. Any one of the sentences above might make a good opening sentence for a whole paragraph. Take the second sentence for example:

Watching television takes time away from other things. (first piece of evidence) For example, all those hours people spend sitting in front of the tube, they could be working on building a chair or fixing the roof. *(second piece of evidence)* Maybe the laundry needs to be done, but because people watch television, they may end up not having time to do it. Then Monday comes around again and they have no socks to wear to work — all because they couldn't stand to miss that episode of "The Sopranos." *(third piece of evidence)* Someone could be writing a letter to a friend in Boston who hasn't been heard from or written to for months. *(fourth piece of evidence)* Or maybe someone misses the opportunity to take in a beautiful day in the park because s/he had to see "Maury." They'll repeat "Maury," but this beautiful day only comes around once. Watching television definitely keeps people from getting things done.

The primary evidence the author uses here is that of probable illustrations taken from life experience, largely anecdotal. Always *supply evidence.* Three examples or illustrations of your idea per paragraph is a useful number. Four is OK, but stop there. Don't go on and on about a single point. You don't have time. In order for a typical test essay to be fully developed, it should have about five paragraphs, organized in the following manner:

Introduction: A paragraph that illustrates your opinion (thesis) on an issue and introduces your position with three general ideas that support your thesis.

Development: Three middle paragraphs that prove your position from different angles, using evidence from real life and knowledge. Each paragraph in the middle should support each of the three ideas you started out with in Paragraph 1.

Conclusion: The last paragraph, which sums up your position and adds one final reminder of what the issue was, perhaps points to a solution:

> So, television takes away from the quality of life and is therefore bad for human beings. We should be watching the sun, the sky, the birds, and each other, not the "boob tube."

Write a paragraph using this sentence as your focus:

> "Television takes valuable time away from our loved ones."

Check for Logic

Make sure that you present your argument in a logical manner. If you have not, you may not have proven your point. Your conclusion must follow from a logical set of premises.

Once again, here is a list of typical fallacies that writers may fall into.

- **Either/or** — The writer assumes that only two opposing possibilities may be attained: "Either this . . . , or this . . . ."

- **Oversimplification** — The writer simplifies the subject: "Only the rich are happy."

- **Begging the question** — The writer assumes he has proved something that needs to be proven: "People who go to college always attain good jobs."

- **Ignoring the issue** — The writer argues against the truth of an issue due to its conclusion: "John is a good boy and therefore did not rob the store."

- **Arguing against a person, not an idea** — The writer argues that somebody's idea has no merit because s/he is immoral or personally stupid: "Eric will fail out of school because he is not doing well in gym class."

- **Non sequitur** — The writer leaps to the wrong conclusion: "Jake is from Canada; he must play hockey."

- **Drawing the wrong conclusion from a sequence** — The author attributes the outcome to the wrong reasons: "Betty married at a young age to an older man and now has three children and is therefore a housewife."

Polishing and Editing Your Essay

If the unit of work for revising is the paragraph, the unit of work for editing is the sentence. In *the last 5 to 10 minutes*, check your paper for mistakes in editing. To help you in this task, follow our checklist.

Polishing Checklist

- Are all your sentences *really* sentences, or have you written some fragments or run-on sentences?

- Are you using your vocabulary correctly?

- Have you used some word that seems colloquial or informal?

- Did you leave out punctuation anywhere? Did you capitalize correctly? Did you check for commas, periods, and quotation marks?

Proofreading

In the last three to five minutes, read your essay word for word, first forward and then backward, reading from the end to the beginning. Doing so can help you find errors that you may have missed by having read forward only.

Strategies for the Photo Prompt Story

The first writing assignment on the HSPA will require you to use your imagination to write a story based on a given photograph. Unlike the open-ended questions or the persuasive writing assignment, this assignment requires speculation and creativity rather than attention to proving one's points. However, this freedom is not a license to forget everything you have learned about clearly organized, coherent writing.

Once you have had an opportunity to see the photo, try to come up with some aspect of it that intrigues or interests you; let your story grow from what you find interesting. Don't worry about picking the "wrong" or "right" story to tell. The trained scorers of this assignment are looking to see if you can use a little imagination, and combine it with a reasonable amount of storytelling skills. This assignment is not the place for avant-garde, "stream of consciousness" writing; it is best to allow the events in your story to move chronologically and naturally, in a traditional narrative structure. You may wish to use the pages provided for prewriting to jot down notes or ideas, or to write a rough draft.

After you have come up with the basic idea for your story and an outline of the progression of events, start filling in some details. The scorers will be reading to see if you can elaborate on important points in the narrative. Just like with the more "academic" writing assignments, you should use the writing process. However, whereas in the essays you need to polish and edit to make sure the points you wanted to make are convincing, in this assignment you need to make sure that the events and details you provide add up to a good story.

Finally, you will need to proofread your story and make any technical corrections that may be necessary. You may wish to follow the polishing/editing recommendations for essays provided in this chapter. During the test, you will be given a copy of the Revising/Editing guide to help polish your assignment.

NEW JERSEY

HSPA

High School Proficiency Assessment in

Language Arts

CHAPTER 3

Review of Standard Written English

REVIEW OF STANDARD WRITTEN ENGLISH

Even though we are constantly surrounded by the English language, many of us are unsure of how to use standard written English properly. Students continually question their ability to recognize correct grammar and usage.

When answering HSPA Language Arts questions, you must be careful not to repeat the common errors that crop up in written English. This review will make you aware of these various errors.

The following pitfalls are the most common errors that are made in writing. By keeping these frequently repeated mistakes in mind when completing the multiple-choice, open-ended, and essay questions in the Language Arts exam, you will be able to identify all the errors quickly and easily.

Section 1: Sentence Fragments

NO: A tree as old as your father.
A sentence fragment does not have enough in it to make it a complete thought. It is usually missing a subject or a verb.

YES: The tree is as old as your father.

Section 2: Run-on Sentences

NO: It was a pleasant drive the sun was shining.
A run-on sentence is a sentence with too much in it. It usually contains two complete sentences separated by a comma, or two complete sentences merged together.

YES: It was a pleasant drive because the sun was shining.

NO: Talk softly, someone is listening.
Sometimes a writer will try to correct a run-on sentence by inserting a comma between the clauses, but this creates another error, a comma splice. The following examples illustrate various ways to correct the comma splice.

YES: Talk softly; someone is listening.

or

Talk softly because someone is listening.

Exercise: Sentence Fragments/Run-on Sentences

> **DIRECTIONS:** The following sentences may be either run-on sentences or sentence fragments. Make any necessary corrections.

1. After the rain stopped.

2. Mow the lawn, it is much too long.

3. The settlement you reached it seems fair.

4. When I read, especially at night. My eyes get tired.

5. It was impossible to get through on the phone, the lines were down because of the storm.

Section 3: Short Sentences/Wordiness

Effective writing means concise writing. Wordiness, on the other hand, decreases the clarity of expression by cluttering sentences with unnecessary words. Of course, all short sentences are not better than long ones simply because they are brief. As long as a word serves a function, it should remain in the sentence. However, repetition of words, sounds, and phrases should be used only for emphasis or other stylistic reasons. Editing your writing will reduce its bulk. Notice the difference in impact between the first and second sentences in the following pairs.

NO: The medical exam that he gave me was entirely complete.

YES: The medical exam he gave me was complete.

NO: Larry asked his friend John, who was a good, old friend, if he would join him and go along with him to see the foreign film made in Japan.

YES: Larry asked his good, old friend John if he would join him in seeing the Japanese film.

NO: I was absolutely, totally happy with the present that my parents gave to me at 7 a.m. on the morning of my birthday.

YES: I was totally happy with the present my parents gave me on the morning of my birthday.

NO: It seems perfectly clear to me that although he went and got permission from the professor, he still should not have played that awful, terrible joke on the dean.

YES: It seems clear to me that although he got permission from the professor, he still should not have played that terrible joke on the dean.

NO: He went to England by means of a long boat.

YES: He went to England by boat.

NO: It will be our aim to ensure proper health care for each and every one of the people in the United States.

YES: Our aim will be to ensure proper health care for all Americans.

Exercise: Short Sentences/Wordiness

> **DIRECTIONS:** Through revision, improve the following sentences.

1. He graduated college. In no time he found a job. Soon after he rented an apartment. He was very happy.

2. The book that she lent me was lengthy. It was boring. I wouldn't recommend it to anyone. There was nothing about the book that I enjoyed.

3. It was raining. We expected to go on a picnic. Now our plans are ruined. We have nothing to do.

4. Whenever anyone telephoned her to ask her for help with their homework she always obliged right away.

5. She liked to paint. She was quite good. Materials are expensive. She can't afford them.

Section 4: Misplaced Modifiers

NO: Harold watched the painter gaping in astonishment.
The dangling participle is an error that results in an unclear sentence. The participle should appear immediately before or after the subject of the sentence.

YES: Gaping in astonishment, Harold watched the painter.

NO: On correcting the test, his errors became apparent.
Many modifiers cause confusion when they are out of place.

YES: His errors became apparent when the test was corrected.

NO: Jane almost polished the plate until it shined.
Words such as *almost, only, just, even, nearly, hardly, not,*
and *merely* must appear immediately before the word they
modify or they will cause confusion.

YES: Jane polished the plate until it almost shined.

Exercise: Misplaced Modifiers

> **DIRECTIONS:** The following group of sentences may contain misplaced
> modifiers. Make any necessary corrections.

1. I saw a stray dog riding the bus this afternoon.

2. The clothing was given to the poor in large packages.

3. I found five dollars eating lunch in the park.

4. We saw two girls riding bicycles from our car.

5. Reading my book quietly, I jumped up when the car crashed.

Section 5: Parallel Structure

NO: The janitor stopped, listened a moment, then he locked the
door.
When ideas are similar, they should be expressed in similar
forms. When elements of a sentence are similar, they too
should appear in similar form.

YES: The janitor stopped, listened a moment, then locked the door.

Exercise: Parallel Structure

> **DIRECTIONS:** The following group of sentences may contain errors in
> parallel structure. Make any necessary corrections.

1. In the summer I usually like swimming and to water-ski.

2. The professor explained the cause, effect, and the results.

3. Mary read the book, studied the examples, and takes the test.

4. Mark watched the way John started the car, and how he left the curb.

5. They bought the house because of location and its affordability.

Section 6: Phrases and Clauses

Phrases

> All this time the Guard was looking *at her*, first *through a telescope*, then *through a microscope,* and then *through an opera-glass. At last* he said, "You're travelling the wrong way," and shut up the window and went away.
>
> "So young a child," said the gentleman *sitting opposite to her* (he was dressed *in white paper),* "ought to know which way she's going, even if she doesn't know her own name!"
>
> A Goat, that was sitting *next to the gentleman in white,* shut his eyes and said in a loud voice, "She ought to know her way *to the ticket-office,* even if she doesn't know her alphabet!"
>
> – Lewis Carroll, *Through the Looking Glass*

All the italicized groups of words are **phrases**. Phrases fill in many of the details that make a sentence interesting. For example, the sentence "We sat." could turn into any of the following by the addition of phrases:

> We sat for hours, *looking at the painting*.
> On the cliffs by the sea we sat, *watching the sunset*.
> We sat by Amelia *at the restaurant*.

A **phrase** is a group of connected words without a subject or predicate. A **prepositional phrase** begins with a preposition, and contains a noun and its modifiers. Some examples are:

> Take me *to the opera*.
> I think Mark is *in his room*.
> What is *in the box* that came *from Hawaii*?
> George works best *under pressure*.
> *After the movie*, let's drive *by the river*.

The noun in a prepositional phrase is called the **object of the preposition**. A prepositional phrase can be used as an adjective.

> The woman *on the phone* is Jane.
> The mysteries *of outer space* are waiting for us.

Henry felt like the Sword *of Damocles* was hanging over his head.

A prepositional phrase can also be used as an adverb.

Anthony was caught *between the horns of a dilemma.*
A large rabbit dove *under the ground.*
Carol lifted the weight *with apparent ease.*
Without doubt, the council decided for the best.

A prepositional phrase can be used as a noun as well.

In the evening is as good a time as any.

A **gerund phrase** contains a gerund and its modifiers. It is always used as a noun.

Reading blueprints is not as easy as it sounds.
Thoreau placed great value on *living simply.*
Wandering in and out of stores is Harriet's favorite way of passing time.
Living well is the best revenge.
Leaving at night helped us avoid the traffic. (gerund phrase as subject)
They accused him of *robbing the bank.* (gerund phrase as the object of the preposition *of*)
Exercising regularly is *seizing an opportunity to keep healthy.* (gerund phrase as subject and as predicate nominative)

An **infinitive phrase** contains an infinitive and its modifiers. It can also be used as a noun, adjective, or adverb.

To know him is *to know his brother.* (noun)
A waiter's job is *to serve a table.* (noun)
It's important to have good language *to suit the occasion.* (adjective)
Tom brought a book *to lend me.* (adjective)
We'll have to run *to catch the train.* (adverb)
No one had time *to complete the extra-credit problem.* (infinitive phrase used as an adjective modifying the noun *time*)
We managed *to arrive on time.* (infinitive phrase used as an adverb modifying the verb *manage*)
We hope *to win the race.* (infinitive phrase used as an object of the verb)

The **present infinitive** also expresses the future time.

We hope *now* to win the race *in the future.*

A **participial phrase** contains a participle and its modifiers. It is used as an adjective to modify a noun or a pronoun.

> The gentleman *standing in the aisle* is the owner.
> *Having said his piece*, he sat down.
> The fisherman, *weathered by experience*, calmly took the line.
> *Walking the balance beam*, she was extremely careful. (The participial phrase modifies *she. Balance beam* is the direct object of the participle *walking*.)
> *Missing the bus by a second*, we decided to take a taxi. (The participial phrase modifies *we. Bus* is the object of the participle *missing*.)
> *Running into the house*, Mary tripped on the rug. (*Running into the house* is the participial phrase. But the prepositional phrase *into the house* is also a part. It modifies the participle *running*. The participial phrase modifies *Mary. House* is the object of the preposition *into*.)

The incorrect use of the participial phrase results in a stylistic error called the **dangling modifier**. For further information on these phrases, see Section 4, "Misplaced Modifiers."

Exercise: Phrases

> **DIRECTIONS:** In the following sentences, label the **prepositional phrase** (PR), the **infinitive phrase** (I), the **participle phrase** (P), and the **gerund phrase** (G). In the prepositional phrases, identify the **object of the preposition** (OP).

1. The police set out to solve the crime and to maintain justice.

2. The woman on the billboard over there is a famous athlete.

3. The man, having painted the house, took a rest.

4. Staying in shape is not as difficult as it appears.

5. James solved the problem with pure logic.

Clauses

A **clause** differs from a phrase in that it has a subject and a predicate.

PHRASE: We're planning a trip *to the museum.*

CLAUSE: We're planning a trip *so we can see the museum.*

PHRASE: *After a swim*, we'll have lunch.

CLAUSE: *After we swim*, we'll have lunch.

PHRASE: Bill told them *during dinner.*

CLAUSE: Bill told them *while they were eating dinner.*

PHRASE: *In the box* he found some old letters.

CLAUSE: *When he looked in the box*, he found some old letters.

PHRASE: Harriet laughed *at the comedian.*

CLAUSE: Harriet laughed *whenever the comedian opened his mouth.*

Often a **relative pronoun** like *that, which, who, whom,* or *whoever* will act as the subject of a clause.

> Tell me *who* was singing.
> Everyone *who* signed the sheet is eligible.
> Arnold knew something *that* was generally unknown.
> Do you remember *which* kind is better?
> Give it to *whoever* has the most need.

In introductory clauses, the use of *that* and *which* often presents a problem for the writer. The difference is simple: If the clause is essential to the meaning of the sentence, use *that*. If the clause is not essential to the meaning of the sentence, use *which* and set off the clause with commas.

THAT: The book that contained the formula was missing. (It is essential that the formula is in the missing book.)

WHICH: The book, which contained the formula, was missing. (It is only essential that the book is missing.)

THAT: We saw a movie that lasted two hours. (The length of the film is important.)

WHICH:	We saw a movie, which lasted two hours. (The length of the film is less important.)
THAT:	The car that Al was driving got a flat tire. (Out of several cars, Al's car was the one to get a flat tire.)
WHICH:	The car, which Al was driving, got a flat tire. (This car got a flat tire and, incidentally, Al was driving.)
THAT:	The titles that are underlined will be printed in italics. (Only the underlined titles will be printed in italics. The rest of the titles will not.)
WHICH:	The titles, which are underlined, will be printed in italics. (All of the titles are underlined, and they will all be printed in italics.)
THAT:	Alan owns a boat that sailed around the world. (Alan's boat sailed around the world.)
WHICH:	Alan owns a boat, which sailed around the world. (The fact that it sailed around the world is incidental.)

Exercise: Clauses

DIRECTIONS: In the following sentences, determine whether the italicized portion is a **phrase** or a **clause**.

1. The girl *in the red dress* is my sister.

2. They left the house early *so they could get a good seat in the theater*.

3. John moved the dresser *next to the door*.

4. Everyone *who attended the meeting is a member*.

5. We all knew *that was the truth*.

Section 7: Subject-Verb Agreement

NO: The arrival of many friends promise good times.

Always remember to make the verb agree with the subject of the sentence. Be wary of the words that come between the subject and the verb. They may distract you.

YES: The *arrival* of many friends *promises* good times.

NO: Into the darkness stares her black cats.

Don't be fooled by sentences where the subject follows the verb. Be especially careful to determine the subject and make it agree with the verb.

YES: Into the darkness *stares* her black *cat.*

NO: Either the principal or the football coach usually attend the dance.

When singular subjects are joined by *either . . . or, neither . . . nor,* or *nor,* the verb is also singular.

YES: Either the principal or the football *coach* usually *attends* the dance.

NO: Neither the *cat* nor the *dogs* is eating today.

If one of the subjects is plural and one is singular, make the verb agree with the subject nearest to it.

YES: Neither the cat nor the *dogs are* eating today.

NO: Politics are a noun.

Remember that a word used as the title of a particular work, even if it is plural, requires a singular verb.

YES: Politics is a noun.

Exercise: Subject-Verb Agreement

> **DIRECTIONS:** The following sentences may contain errors in subject-verb agreement. Make any necessary corrections.

1. Either her mother or her father usually drive her to school on rainy days.

2. There is, if I calculated right, $200 left in my bank account.

3. Mary, and her friends, was late for the test.

4. Economics are a major taught in many colleges.

5. The first years of high school is the most difficult.

Section 8: Comparison of Adjectives

NO: That was the most bravest thing he ever did.
Do not combine two superlatives.

YES: That was the *bravest* thing he ever did.

NO: Mary was more friendlier than Susan.
Do not combine two comparatives.

YES: Mary was *friendlier* than Susan.

NO: I can buy either the shirt or the scarf. The shirt is most expensive.
The comparative should be used when only two things are being compared.

YES: I can buy either the shirt or the scarf. The shirt is *more* expensive.

Exercise: Comparison of Adjectives

DIRECTIONS: In the following sentences, make the changes indicated in the parentheses. Also indicate if the comparative or superlative form is an adverb or an adjective.

1. He was sad to leave. (superlative)

2. She ran as fast as the others on the team. (comparative)

3. Throughout school, they were good in math. (superlative)

4. This class is as interesting as the European history class. (comparative)

5. He arrived as soon as I did. (comparative)

Section 9: Pronouns

Pronouns are the simple, everyday words used to refer to people, places, or things that have already been mentioned, such as *him, she, me, it,* or to indefinite people, places, things, or qualities, such as *who, where, this,* or *somebody.* They usually replace some noun and make an expression concise. There are only about fifty pronouns in the English language and most are short words; however, they can be difficult to use correctly.

One reason these words may be so difficult to use properly is their frequency of occurrence. Of the twenty-five most commonly used words in the English language, ten are pronouns.

Perhaps it is due to their frequent usage that pronouns have acquired a variety of distinctive functions. Although pronouns are dissimilar in the ways they may or may not be used, they have two things in common. The first is their ability to stand alone, or "stand in" for nouns. The second is that they all have little specific meaning. Whatever meaning they have derives from the context in which they are found. Some pronouns that modify other words are also adjectives. In this chapter, we will mainly speak of pronouns that stand alone — that take the place either of a definite noun or of an unknown or uncertain noun. When we use pronouns as adjectives in examples in this section, they are marked (a.).

> *Whom* are *you* speaking to?
> *That* is *my* (a.) hat *you* are holding in *your* (a.) hand.
> Marsha *herself* (a.) told *them all* (a.) about *what* happened to *her when it* started to rain.
> *Somebody* had to let the *others* know *that she* was not to blame.
> *Who, what, where, when,* and *how* are the five words by *which you* can organize *this*.
> *This* is a new kind of information for *me* and *I* regret to *some* (a.) degree *that I* can't be more in touch with *them*.
> *She* doesn't agree with *me*; *that*'s too bad, but *that*'s the way *it* is.
> *I've* had *enough*! If *no one* wants to take care of *it*, *I'll* do *it myself* (a.).
> *It* is not *enough* to think of *me*; *you* should send *me* a letter *when you* do.
> *I* wonder *what* is in *it*.

All the italicized words in the preceding sentences are pronouns. Traditionally, pronouns are divided into six groups; each group has its own name, definition, and special functions. These categories are helpful in learning how to recognize the different kinds of pronouns and how to use them correctly, since they come in such a wide variety of forms.

Personal Pronouns

Because of their many forms, this can be a troublesome group.

Case

NUMBER	PERSON	SUBJECT	OBJECT	POSSESSIVE	POSSESSIVE ADJECTIVE
Singular	1st person	*I*	*me*	*mine*	*my*
	2nd person	*you*	*you*	*yours*	*your*
	3rd person* (masc.)	*he*	*him*	*his*	*his*
	(fem.)	*she*	*her*	*hers*	*her*
	(neuter)	*it*	*it*		*its*
Plural	1st	*we*	*us*	*ours*	*our*
	2nd	*you*	*you*	*yours*	*your*
	3rd	*they*	*them*	*theirs*	*their*
		_____saw it.	Let _____.	That's _____.	_____house.

*When a pronoun is used to refer to someone (other than the speaker or the person spoken to), the "third person" is used, and a different form of the pronoun is employed to show the gender of the person referred to. *His, her, him, his*, and *hers* all indicate the masculine or feminine gender. *It* and *its* refer to something to which gender does not apply.

There are three forms of personal pronouns:

1. PERSON: to indicate whether the person is the speaker (1st person), the person being spoken to (2nd person), or the person being spoken about (3rd person).

2. CASE: to show the job the pronoun is performing in the sentence.

3. NUMBER: to indicate whether the word is plural or singular.

Examples of Personal Pronoun Use

> *I* went yesterday to see *her*.
> *You* have *my* (a.) hat, don't *you*?
> *Her* car was formerly *theirs*.
> Between *you* and *me*, I really don't want to go with *him*.
> In *his* opinion, the boating dock is *ours*, not *yours*.
> *They* say *you* can't take *it* with *you*.
> Won't *you* walk down to *his* garden with *them*?

Errors to Avoid — Pronoun Case

When a compound subject or object includes a pronoun, be sure that the case chosen is in agreement with the pronoun's place in the sentence — a subject case pronoun is used as the subject of the verb, an object case pronoun is used as the object, etc. The same rule of agreement is true when using an appositive (a word or words with the same meaning as the pronoun); the pronoun must be in the same case form as the word it renames.

Compounds

Both Mary and *he* (NOT *him*) have seen that movie. (subject — "Mary and he")

Last year the team elected both Jane and *me* (NOT *I*). (object — "Jane and me")

Could you wait for my brother and *me* (NOT *I*)? (object of a preposition — "My brother and me")

A trip to Europe appealed to Susan and *him* (NOT *he*). (object of a preposition — "Susan and him")

There has always been a great friendship between you and *me* (NOT *I*). (object of a preposition — "You and me")

Mrs. Williams and *I* (NOT *me*) will direct the chorus. (subject — "Mrs. Williams and I")

Appositions

Words with the same meaning as the pronoun.

We Americans value freedom. (subject)

They invited *us* (NOT *we*) cheerleaders. (object)

Let's you and *me* (NOT *I*) go together. (object)

Both players, James and *he* (NOT *him*), could be stars. (subject)

Our school sent two delegates, Mark and *him* (NOT *he*). (object)

It is not for *we* writers to determine editorial policy. (subject)

Will you give your decision to *us* applicants soon? (object)

Relative Pronouns — Interior Sentences (Clauses)

Relative pronouns play the part of the subject or object in sentences within sentences (clauses). They often refer to nouns that have preceded them, making the sentence more compact.

NO: The flower — the flower was yellow — made her smile.

YES: The flower, *which* was yellow, made her smile.

NO: The girl — the girl lived down the block — loved him.

YES: The girl *who* lived down the block loved him.

Sometimes their reference is indefinite.

> I wonder *what* happened. (The event that occurred is uncertain.)
> I'll call *whomever* you want. (The people to be called are un-
> known.)

Who (for persons), *that* (for persons and things), and *which* (for things) are the most common pronouns of this type.

Who can cause problems because it changes form depending on the part it plays in the interior sentence (clause).

Subject	Object	Possessive
who	whom	whose

> Mr. Jackson, *who* is my friend, called yesterday. (subject)
> Mr. Jackson, *whom* I know well, called yesterday. (object)
> Mr. Jackson, *whose* friendship is important to me, called yester-
> day. (possessive)

Interrogative Pronouns — Questions

These pronouns are easy to recognize because they always introduce either direct or indirect questions. The words just discussed as relative pronouns are called **interrogative pronouns** when they introduce a question: *who, what, that, which, whom, whose, whoever, whichever,* and *whatever.*

> *Who* is at the door? (refers to a person)
> *What* do you want from me? (refers to a thing)
> *Which* (flavor) do you want? (refers to a thing)
> *Which* (a.) boy won the match? (refers to a person)
> *Whatever* you mean by "liberal education," I don't know.
> Is *that* what you meant to say?
> *Whom* did you telephone last night?

Sometimes an interrogative is not recognized when it is used indirectly inside another sentence.

> She wondered *who* was at the door.
> Samuel asked them *what* they wanted.
> He didn't know if he would ever find out *what* happened.
> I couldn't guess *which* they would choose.

Demonstrative Pronouns — Pointers

This, *that*, *these*, and *those* are the most common words used as pronouns to point to someone or something clearly expressed or implied.

> *That* is the apple I wanted. (subject)
> Bring me *those*, please. (object)
> I must tell him *that*. (object)
> *These* are the ones I've been looking for. (subject)
> *That* really made me mad! (subject)
> "*This* above all, to thine own self be true." (subject)
> Give *this* to her for me. (object)

Such or *so* may also serve as pointing pronouns.

> *Such* was his fate. (subject)
> He resented Jerry and told him *so*. (object)

These same words are often used as adjectives, and at first glance it is easy to classify them only as adjectives, forgetting that they also take the place of nouns and serve as pronouns.

> *That* apple is the one I want. (adjective describing "apple")
> Bring me *those* books, please. (adjective describing "books")
> I must tell him *that* story. (adjective describing "story")
> It was *such* a tiring day. (adjective describing "day")
> She was *so* happy. (adjective describing "happy")

Indefinite Pronouns

This group of pronouns acquired its name because the reference (the noun for which they are standing in) is indefinite.

Indefinite persons or things: (all singular pronouns)

everybody	everyone
somebody	someone
anybody	anyone
nobody	no one

Everybody joined in the chorus.
No one took less than he did.
Is *anyone* here?
I hope *someone* answers my calls.

Indefinite quantities:

each	either	
another	some	all
several	few	both
least	little	less
lots	plenty	many
other	more	most

Much has been said on the subject of delinquency.
She took *several* for herself.
It is *less* than I'd bargained for.
Dallas or Houston — *either* would be fine for me.
There are *plenty* of people who want your job.
Many are called, but *few* are chosen.
The *most* we can expect is to see her next week.
Each must chart his own course.

The biggest problem encountered with these pronouns is in trying to decide if they are singular or plural. See "Agreement" section for a discussion of this problem.

Reflexive Pronouns

These are the pronouns that end in *"self"* or *"selves."*

myself	yourself	yourselves
himself	herself	itself
ourselves	themselves	

Their main purpose is to reflect back on the subject of a sentence.

She cut *herself.* (object, refers to "she")
I bought *myself* a new dress. (object, refers to "I")
You are just not *yourself* today. (object, refers to "you")
They consider *themselves* lucky. (object, refers to "they")
Give *yourself* a treat; go to the ice cream shop. (object, refers to "you" understood)
After that dust storm I washed *myself* very well. (object, refers to "I")

They also provide emphasis. When they serve this purpose, they should appear at the end of the sentence.

We will triumph over this outrage *ourselves.*
I will go to the ticket office *myself.*

She will tell it to him *herself.*
You *yourself* must discover the meaning.
I suppose I will have to do it *myself.*

Errors to Avoid — Reflexive Pronouns

Do not use the reflexive in place of the shorter personal pronoun.

NO: Both Sandy and *myself* plan to go.

YES: Both Sandy and *I* plan to go.

NO: *Yourself* will take on the challenges of college.

YES: *You* will take on the challenges of college.

NO: Either James or *yourself* will paint the mural.

YES: Either James or *you* will paint the mural.

Watch out for careless use of the pronoun form.

NO: George *hisself* told me it was true.

YES: George *himself* told me it was true.

NO: They washed the car *theirselves.*

YES: They washed the car *themselves.*

Notice that the reflexive pronouns are not set off by commas.

NO: Mary, *herself*, gave him the diploma.

YES: Mary *herself* gave him the diploma.

NO: I will do it, *myself.*

YES: I will do it *myself.*

Case — The Function of the Pronoun in a Sentence

By far the pronouns with which we are apt to make the most mistakes are those that change their form when they play different parts in a sentence — the personal pronouns and the relative pronoun *who.* A careful study of the peculiarities of these changes is necessary to avoid the mistakes associated with their use.

Subject Case (used mainly when the pronoun is a subject)

Use the **subject case** (*I, we, you, he, she, it, they, who,* and *whoever*) for the following purposes:

1. *As a subject or a repeated subject:*

    NO: Mrs. Jones and *me* left early yesterday.

    YES: Mrs. Jones and *I* left early yesterday.

    ***

    NO: I know *whom* that is.

    YES: I know *who* that is. (subject of "is")

    ***

    NO: *Us* girls always go out together.

    YES: *We* girls always go out together. ("girls" is the subject; "we" repeats it)

    Watch out for a parenthetical expression (an expression that is not central to the meaning of the sentence). It looks like a subject and verb when actually it is the pronoun that is the subject.

    NO: Larry is the one *whom* we know will do the best job.

    YES: Larry is the one *who* we know will do the best job. (Do not be misled by "we know"; *who* is the subject of the verb "will do.")

    ***

    NO: It was Jim and Gretchen *whom* I think were there.

    YES: It was Jim and Gretchen *who* I think were there. (Disregard "I think"; *who* is the subject of *were.*)

2. *Following the verb "to be" when it has a subject:*

    This is a part of the language that appears to be changing. It is a good example of how the grammar of a language follows speech and not the other way around. The traditional guideline has been that a pronoun following a form of "be" must be in the same case as the word before the verb.

    > It is *I*. ("It" is the subject.)
    > I thought it was *she*. ("it" is the subject.)
    > Was it *they* who arrived late? ("it" is the subject.)

    Our ear tells us that in informal conversation "It is I" would sound too formal, so instead we tend to say:

It is *me*. (in conversation)
I thought it was *her*. (in conversation)
Was it *them* who arrived late? (in conversation)

In written English, however, it is best to follow the standard of using the subject case after the verb "be" when "be" is preceded by a word in the subject case, even though the pronoun is in the position of an object.

Some more examples that might cause trouble:

NO: Last week, the best students were *you* and *me*.

YES: Last week, the best *students* were *you* and *I*. (refers to "students," subject of "were")

NO: Whenever I hear that knock, I know it must be *him*.

YES: Whenever I hear that knock, I know it must be *he*. (refers to "it," subject of "must be")

NO: The *leaders* of the parade were John, Susan, and *me*.

YES: The leaders of the parade were John, Susan, and *I*. (refers to "leaders," subject of "were")

NO: I am expecting my mother to call. Is that *her*?

YES: I am expecting my *mother* to call. Is that *she*? (refers to "mother," subject of "to call")

3. *As a subject when the verb is omitted* (often after *than* or *as*):

I have known her longer than *he*. ("has known her" is understood)
She sings as well as *I*. ("sing" is understood)
We do just as well in algebra as *they*. ("do" is understood)
He is much better than *I* at such calculations. ("than I am at such calculations" — "am" is understood)

To test whether the subject or the object form is correct, complete the phrase in your mind and it will be obvious.

Object Case (used mainly when the pronoun is an object)

Use the **object case** (*me, us, him, her, it, you, them, whom, whomever*) as follows:

1. *As the direct or indirect object, object of a preposition, or repeated object:*

The postman gave *me* the letter. (indirect object)

Mr. Boone appointed *him* and *me* to clean the room. ("him and me" is the object of "appointed")

They told *us* managers to rewrite the first report. ("managers" is the indirect object of "told"; "us" repeats)

My attorney gave *me* a letter giving *her* power of attorney. ("me" is the indirect object of "gave"; "her" is the indirect object of "giving")

That package is from *me*. (object of "from")

Between *you* and *me*, I'm voting Republican. (object of "between")

Whom were you thinking about? (object of "about")

I know *whom* you asked. (object of "asked")

My teacher gave both of *us*, June and *me*, an "A." ("us" is the object of "of"; "June and me" repeats the object)

2. *As the subject of an infinitive verb:*

I wanted *her* to come.

Janet invited *him* and *me* to attend the conference.

He asked *her* to duplicate the report for the class.

Whom will we ask to lead the group? ("Whom" is the subject of "to lead")

3. *As an object when the verb or preposition is omitted:*

Father told my sister June more about it than (he told) *me*.

The telephone calls were more often for Marilyn than (they were for) *him*.

Did they send them as much candy as (they sent) *us*?

He always gave Susan more than (he gave) *me*.

4. *Following "to be":*

In point number 2, we learned that the subject of an infinitive verb form must be in the object case. The infinitive "to be" is an exception to this rule. Forms of "to be" must have the same case before and after the verb. If the word preceding the verb is in the subject case, the pronoun following must be in the subject case also. (For example, *It is I*.) If the word before the verb is an object, the pronoun following must be objective as well.

We thought the *author* of the note to be *her*.

You expected the *winner* to be *me*.

Mother did not guess *it* to be Julie and *me* at the door.
Had you assumed the *experts* to be *us*?

5. *Subject of a progressive verb form that functions as an adjective (participle — "ing" ending):*

Two kinds of words commonly end in "ing": a **participle**, or a word that looks like a verb but acts like an adjective, and a **gerund**, a word that looks like a verb but acts like a noun. When an "ing" word acts like an adjective, its subject is in the object case.

For example:

Can you imagine *him acting* that way? ("acting" refers to the pronoun and is therefore a participle which takes a subject in the object case, "him")

They watched *me smiling* at all the visitors. ("smiling" refers to the pronoun, which must be objective, "me")

Compare:

Can you imagine *his acting* in that part? (Here the emphasis is on "acting"; "his" refers to "acting" which is functioning as a noun (it is a gerund) and takes the possessive case.)

It was *my smiling* that won the contest. (Emphasis is on "smiling" — it is playing the part of a noun and so takes a possessive case pronoun, "my.")

Possessive Case

Use the **possessive adjective** case (*my, our, your, her, his, its, their, whose*) in the following situations:

1. *To indicate possession,* classification of something, or connection. Possession is the most common.

    I borrowed *her* car. (The car belongs to her.)
    Come over to *our* house. (The house belongs to us.)
    That is Jane's and *my* report. (The report belongs to us.)
    It is *anyone's* guess.
    Whose coat is this?
    The plant needs water; *its* leaves are fading.

2. *Preceding a verb acting as a noun (gerund):*

    Our leaving early helped end the party.
    Whose testifying will you believe?

His reading was excessive.

Don't you think *her* playing astounded them?

Since there are no possessive forms for the demonstrative pronouns *that*, *this*, *these*, and *those*, they do not change form before a gerund.

NO: What are the chances of *that's* being painted today?

YES: What are the chances of *that* being painted today?

Use the **possessive case** (*mine, ours, yours, hers, his, its, theirs, whose*) in the following situations:

In any role a noun might play — a subject, object, or complement with a possessive meaning.

> *Hers* was an exciting career. ("Hers" is the subject of "was")
>
> Can you tell me *whose* this is? ("whose" is the complement of "is")
>
> He is a friend of *mine*. ("mine" is the object of the preposition "of")
>
> We borrowed *theirs* last week; it is only right that they should use *ours* this week. ("theirs" is the object of the verb "borrowed"; "ours" is the object of the verb "use")
>
> I thought that was Mary's and *his*. ("Mary's and his" is the complement of the verb "was")

It and There — Expletives

Dictionaries will tell you that *it* and *there* are pronouns, but they are somewhat different from pronouns. They have even less meaning than the sometimes vague or indefinite pronouns. Because they provide so little information, their sole function is to fill space, to provide a formal subject for a sentence.

It — Impersonal

> *It's* cold outside. (what is "it"?)
>
> *It's* March 3.
>
> What is this? *It's* my comb.
>
> *It's* ten after three.
>
> *It's* a twenty-minute walk to the grocery store.
>
> *It* seems warmer than yesterday.
>
> I know *it* gets crowded here at noon.

It — Anticipatory

Sometimes *it* fills the subject position while the actual subject appears later in the sentence. The italicized sections of the following sentences are the actual subjects.

> It's surprising *how handsome he is.*
> It's interesting *to know your background.*
> It's curious *that Mary paints so well.*
> It's hard *to keep reading this.*
> It's pleasant *to study words.*
> It's good *knowing you are waiting for me.*

Notice how *there* has no meaning but only fills the space of the subject.

> *There* are three of us watching you.
> *There* is lightning outside.
> *There* are many ways to peel an onion.
> *There* are only a few teachers who teach well.
> *There's* a sale at Target.
> *There* shall come a time when all this will end.

There is also often used as an adverb. If *there* is an expletive (space-filler), it is likely to be accompanied by "a." If it is accompanied by "the," it is probably an adverb and not a space-filler.

> *There's* a place I'd like to visit. (space-filler)
> *There's* the place I'd like to visit. (adverb referring to "is")
> *There's* a girl in the corner. (space-filler)
> *There's* the girl in the corner. (adverb referring to "is")

Agreement Between the Pronoun and the Word(s) It Refers To

A pronoun usually takes the place of some noun. The noun (or group of words that works as a noun) for which the pronoun stands in is called the **antecedent**. It usually comes before the pronoun in the sentence or the paragraph. It is important to remember that the pronoun and the word(s) it refers to have to "agree." If the antecedent is plural, the pronoun should be plural; if the antecedent is singular, the pronoun must also be. The gender and person must also be consistent.

> I heard *one dog* barking *his* loudest.
> I heard *three dogs* barking *their* loudest.
> The *woman* raised *her* hand.
> The *children* raised *their* hands.
> The *man* read *his* newspaper.

Exercise: Pronouns

A. Relative Pronouns

> **DIRECTIONS:** Complete the following sentences with a relative pronoun.

1. The man, _____ is standing in line, is a famous author.

2. She looks sad. I wonder _____ news she received.

3. The house, _____ was white, has been abandoned.

4. _____ one you chose will satisfy me.

5. I'll sing _____ you want.

B. Relative Pronouns

> **DIRECTIONS:** "Who and Whom." In the following sentences choose the correct form of the pronoun given in the parentheses.

1. It's Susan from (who, whom) I received the assignment.

2. I must see the teacher (who, whom) I spoke with last week.

3. She is a girl (who, whom) I know very well.

4. I can't remember (who, whom) I met yesterday.

5. If you know (who, whom) sent the letter, please give me a name and an address.

C. Interrogative and Demonstrative Pronouns

> **DIRECTIONS:** Write five sentences using different interrogative pronouns. Then do the same exercise for demonstrative pronouns. In some of your sentences try using the pronouns in their less common role. Use them indirectly inside a sentence (interrogative pronoun) and as adjectives (demonstrative pronoun).

D. Reflexive Pronouns

> **DIRECTIONS:** Complete the following sentences with the appropriate reflexive pronoun. Also note which pronoun the "reflector" is an object of.

1. We found _____ out of money.

2. I _____ will complete the project.

3. Give _____ the time needed.

4. The play, by _____, was quite good.

5. They will give it to him _____.

E. Reflexive Pronouns

DIRECTIONS: In the following sentences make the necessary corrections.

1. Both James and themselves went to the beach.

2. Jack, himself, read the speech.

3. Myself will unload the car.

4. They finished the painting theirselves.

5. He mowed the lawn, hisself.

F. Personal Pronouns

DIRECTIONS: In the following sentences choose the correct form of the pronoun given in the parentheses.

1. Both Peter and (I, me) went to the movies.

2. They missed the train because of (he, him).

3. (We, Us) soldiers must be ready for combat at all times.

4. You and (I, me) have always understood each other.

5. I don't know if it was (she, her) who was in the theater yesterday.

6. Susan and (he, him) have met before.

7. Neither Jack nor (they, them) will be going on vacation this summer.

8. We sing just as well as (they, them).

9. Do (we, us) officers have to attend the convention?

10. I am older than (she, her).

11. Mr. Grey and (I, me) will paint the scenery for the play.

12. Paul questioned (she, her) and (I, me) about the accident.

13. Both students, Mark and (he, him), were suspended from school.

14. They told (us, we) to clean the house.

G. Possessive Pronouns

DIRECTIONS: Complete the following sentences with an appropriate possessive pronoun.

1. _____ car is this?

2. That is _____ dress in the closet.

3. What are the chances of _____ being finished tomorrow?

4. _____ intelligence was staggering.

5. They are relatives of _____.

H. Expletives

DIRECTIONS: Complete the following sentences with the correct expletive.

1. _____ the first day of March.

2. _____ are only a few chances left.

3. _____ time to finish the game.

4. _____ looks like rain.

5. _____ interesting to read history.

I. Pronouns

DIRECTIONS: Complete the following sentences with an appropriate pronoun.

1. The girl picked up _____ books.

2. The detectives finished _____ case.

3. I saw a beaver building _____ nest.

4. The villagers had _____ meetings on Wednesdays.

5. John left _____ key at home.

Section 10: Conjunctions

NO: She loved him dearly but not his dog.
   When using a conjunction, be sure that the sentence parts you are joining are in agreement.

YES: *She loved him dearly* but *she did not love his dog.*

NO: They complimented them both for their bravery and they thanked them for their kindness.
   When using conjunctions, a common mistake that is made is to forget that each member of the pair must be followed by the same kind of construction.

YES: They both *complimented them for their bravery* and *thanked them for their kindness.*

NO: While I'm usually interested in Fellini movies, I'd rather not go tonight.
   While refers to time and should not be used as a substitute for *although, and,* or *but.*

YES: *Although* I'm usually interested in Fellini movies, I'd rather not go tonight.

NO: We read in the paper where they are making great strides in DNA research.
   Where refers to a place or location. Be careful not to use it when it does not have this meaning.

YES: We read in the paper *that* they are making great strides in DNA research.

Exercise: Conjunctions

> **DIRECTIONS:** The following group of sentences may contain errors in the use of conjunctions. Make any necessary corrections.

1. John's best assets are his personality and swimming ability.

2. I heard on the radio where the play is closing this week.

3. I was reading the paper and the phone rang.

4. Susan ate vegetables often but not fruits.

5. Please send me an answer to the question or opinions on the project.

Section 11: The Comma

Of all the marks of punctuation, the comma (,) has the most uses. Before you tackle the main principles that guide its usage, be sure that you have an elementary understanding of sentence structure. There are actually only a few rules and conventions to follow when using commas; the rest is common sense. The worst abuse of commas comes from those who over-use them and place them illogically. If you are ever in doubt as to whether or not to use a comma, do not use it.

In a Series

When more than one adjective (an adjective series) describes a noun, use a comma to separate and emphasize each adjective.

> the long, dark passageway
> another confusing, sleepless night
> an elaborate, complex plan
> the beautiful, starry night
> the haunting, melodic sound
> the old, grey, crumpled hat

In these instances, the comma takes the place of "and." To test if the comma is needed, try inserting "and" between the adjectives in question. If it is logical, you should use a comma. The following are examples of adjectives that describe an adjective-noun combination that has come to be thought of almost as one word. In such cases the adjective in front of the adjective-noun combination needs no comma.

a stately oak tree	my worst report card
an exceptional wine glass	a borrowed record player
a successful garage sale	a porcelain dinner plate

If you insert "and" between the adjectives in the above examples, it will not make sense.

The comma is also used to separate words, phrases, and whole ideas (clauses); it still takes the place of "and" when used this way.

> an apple, a pear, a fig, and a banana
> a lovely lady, an indecent dress, and many admirers
> She lowered the shade, closed the curtain, turned off the light, and went to bed.
> John, Frank, and my Uncle Harry all thought it was a questionable theory.

The only question that exists about the use of commas in a series is whether or not one should be used before the final item. Usually "and" or "or" precedes the final item, and many writers do not include the comma before the final "and" or "or." When first learning, however, it is advisable to use the comma because often its omission can be confusing; in such cases as these, for instance:

NO: Would you like to shop at Saks, Lord and Taylor and Bloomingdale's?

NO: He got on his horse, tracked a rabbit and a deer and rode on to Canton.

YES: Would you like to shop at Saks, Lord and Taylor, and Bloomingdale's?

With a Long Introductory Phrase

Usually if a phrase of more than five or six words precedes the subject at the beginning of a sentence, a comma is used to set it off.

> After last night's fiasco at the disco, she couldn't bear the thought of looking at him again.
> Whenever I try to talk about politics, my husband leaves the room.
> When it comes to actual facts, every generation makes the same mistakes as the preceding one.

Provided you have said nothing, they will never guess who you are.

It is not necessary to use a comma with a short sentence.

In January she will go to Switzerland.
After I rest I'll feel better.
At Grandma's we had a big dinner.
During the day no one is home.

If an introductory phrase includes a verb form that is being used as another part of speech (a "verbal"), it must be followed by a comma. Try to make sense of the following sentences without commas.

NO: When eating Mary never looked up from her plate.

YES: When eating, Mary never looked up from her plate.

NO: Because of her desire to follow her faith in James wavered.

YES: Because of her desire to follow, her faith in James wavered.

NO: Having decided to leave Mary James wrote her a letter.

YES: Having decided to leave Mary, James wrote her a letter.

Above all, common sense is the best guideline when trying to decide whether or not to use a comma after an introductory phrase. Does the comma make the meaning more clear? If it does, use it; if not, there is no reason to insert it.

To Separate Sentences with Two Main Ideas (Compound Sentences)

To understand this use of the comma, you need to have studied sentence structure and be able to recognize compound sentences.

When a sentence contains more than two subjects and verbs (clauses), and the two clauses are joined by a connecting word (*and, but, or, yet, for, nor*), use a comma before the connecting word to show that another clause is coming.

I thought I knew the poem by heart, but he showed me three lines I had forgotten.
Are we really interested in helping the children, or are we more concerned with protecting our good names?
He is supposed to leave tomorrow, but who knows if he will be ready to go.

Jim knows you are disappointed, and he has known it for a long time.

If the two parts of the sentence are short and closely related, it is not necessary to use a comma.

He threw the ball and the dog ran after it.
Jane played the piano and Charles danced.

Errors to Avoid

Be careful not to confuse a sentence that has a compound verb and a single subject with a compound sentence. **If the subject is the same for both verbs, there is no need for a comma.**

NO: Charles sent some flowers, and wrote a long letter explaining why he had not been able to come.

NO: Last Thursday we went to the concert with Julia, and afterwards dined at an old Italian restaurant.

NO: For the third time, the teacher explained that the literacy level of high school students was much lower than it had been in previous years, and, this time, wrote the statistics on the board for everyone to see.

To Set Off Interrupting Material

There are so many different kinds of interruptions that can occur in a sentence that a list of them all would be quite lengthy. In general, words and phrases that stop the flow of the sentence or are unnecessary for the main idea are set off by commas. Some examples are:

Abbreviations after names

Did you invite John Paul, Jr., and his sister?
Martha Harris, Ph.D., will be the speaker tonight.

Interjections: An exclamation added without grammatical connection

Oh, I'm so glad to see you.
I tried so hard, alas, to do it.
Hey, let me out of here.
No, I will not let you out.

Direct address

Roy, won't you open the door for the dog?
I can't understand, mother, what you are trying to say.

May I ask, Mr. President, why you called us together?
Hey, lady, watch out for the car!

Tag questions: A question that repeats the helping verb in a negative phrase

I'm really hungry, aren't you?
Jerry looks like his father, doesn't he?
You'll come early, won't you?
We are expected at nine, aren't we?
Mr. Jones can chair the meeting, can't he?

Geographical names and addresses

The concert will be held in Chicago, Illinois, on August 12.
They visited Tours, France, last summer.
The letter was addressed to Ms. Marion Heartwell, 1881 Pine Lane, Palo Alto, California 95824. (No comma is needed before the ZIP code because it is already clearly set off from the state name.)

Transitional words and phrases

On the other hand, I hope he gets better.
In addition, the phone rang six times this afternoon.
I'm, nevertheless, going to the beach on Sunday.
You'll find, therefore, no one is more loyal to me than you.
To tell the truth, I don't know what to believe.

Parenthetical words and phrases

You will become, I believe, a great statesman.
We know, of course, that this is the only thing to do.
In fact, I planted corn last summer.
The Mannes affair was, to put it mildly, a surprise.
Bathing suits, generally speaking, are getting smaller.

Unusual word order

The dress, new and crisp, hung in the closet. (Normal word order: The new, crisp dress hung in the closet.)
Intently, she stared out the window. (Normal word order: She stared intently out the window.)

Nonrestrictive Elements (Not Essential to the Meaning)

Parts of a sentence that modify other parts are sometimes essential to the meaning of the sentence and sometimes not. When a modifying word or group of words is not vital to the meaning of the sentence, it is set off by commas. Since it does not restrict the meaning of the words it modifies, it is called "nonrestrictive." **Modifiers that are essential to the meaning of the sentence are called "restrictive" and are not set off by commas.** *Compare the following pairs of sentences*:

The girl *who wrote the story* is my sister. (essential)

My sister, *the girl who wrote the story*, has always been drawn to adventure. (nonessential)

John Milton's famous poem *"Paradise Lost"* tells a remarkable story. (essential — Milton has written other poems)

Dante's great work, *"The Divine Comedy,"* marked the beginning of the Renaissance and the end of the Dark Ages. (nonessential — Dante wrote only one great work)

The cup *that is on the piano* is the one I want. (essential)

The cup, *which my brother gave me last year,* is on the piano. (nonessential)

My parakeet *Simian* has an extensive vocabulary. (essential — because there are no commas, the writer must have more than one parakeet)

My parakeet, *Simian,* has an extensive vocabulary. (nonessential — the writer must have only one parakeet whose name is Simian)

The people *who arrived late* were not seated. (essential)

George, *who arrived late*, was not seated. (nonessential)

She always listened to her sister *Jean*. (essential — she must have more than one sister)

She always listened to her husband, *Jack*. (nonessential — obviously, she has only one husband)

To Set Off Direct Quotations

Most direct quotes or quoted materials are set off from the rest of the sentence by commas.

"Please read your part more loudly," the director insisted.
"I won't know what to do," said Michael, "if you leave me now."

The teacher said sternly, "I will not dismiss this class until I have silence."

Mark looked up from his work, smiled, and said, "We'll be with you in a moment."

Be careful not to set off indirect quotations or quotes that are used as subjects or complements.

"To be or not to be" is the famous beginning of a soliloquy in Shakespeare's *Hamlet*. (subject)

Back then my favorite song was "*A Summer Place*." (complement)

She said she would never come back. (indirect quote)

"Place two tablespoons of chocolate in this pan" were her first words to her apprentice in the kitchen. (subject)

To Set Off Contrasting Elements

Her intelligence, *not her beauty*, got her the job.

Your plan will take you further from, *rather than closer to*, your destination.

It was a reasonable, *though not appealing*, idea.

He wanted glory, *but found happiness instead*.

James wanted an active, *not a passive*, partner.

In Dates

Both forms of the date are acceptable.

She will arrive on April 6, 1981.

He left on 5 December 1980.

In January, 1967, he handed in his resignation.

In January 1967 he handed in his resignation.

Exercise: The Comma

DIRECTIONS: In the following sentences insert commas wherever necessary. You may also want to note the reason for your choice.

1. However I am willing to reconsider.

2. She descended the long winding staircase.

3. Whenever I practice the violin my family closes the windows.

4. While driving Francis never took his eyes off the road.

5.   The car which I bought last year is in the garage.

6.   "Answer the door" said his mother loudly.

7.   Miss can I ask you for the time?

8.   He was after all an ex-convict.

9.   I'm so bored aren't you?

10. The old tall shady tree is wonderful during the summer.

11. George Gary and Bill were on line early this morning. They bought their tickets read the newspaper and spoke for a while.

12. The author James Grey was awarded the prize.

13. She attended school in London England last year.

14. They said they would do the job.

15. His weight not his height prevented him from competing in the race.

Section 12: The Colon and Semicolon

The Colon

The colon (:) is the sign of a pause about midway in length between the semicolon and the period. It can often be replaced by a comma and sometimes by a period. Although used less frequently now than it was 50 to 75 years ago, the colon is still convenient to use, for it signals to the reader that more information is to come on the subject of concern. The colon can also create a slight dramatic tension.

It is used to introduce a word, phrase, or complete statement (clause) that emphasizes, illustrates, or exemplifies what has already been stated.

> He had only one desire in life: to play baseball.
> The weather that day was the most unusual I'd ever seen: It snowed and rained while the sun was still shining.
> In his speech, the president surprised us by his final point: The conventional grading system would be replaced next year.
> Jean thought of only two things the last half hour of the hike home: a bath and a bed.

Notice that the word following the colon can start with either a capital or a small letter. Use a capital letter if the word following the colon begins another complete sentence. But when the words following the colon are part of the sentence preceding the colon, use a small letter.

May I offer you a suggestion: Don't drive without your seatbelts fastened.

The thought continued to perplex him: Where will I go next?

When introducing a series that illustrates or emphasizes what has already been stated, use the colon.

Only a few of the graduates were able to be there: Jamison, Mearns, Linkley, and Commoner.

For Omar Khayyam, a Persian poet, three things are necessary for a paradise on earth: a loaf of bread, a jug of wine, and his beloved.

In the basement, he kept some equipment for his experiments: the test tubes, some chemical agents, three sunlamps, and the drill.

Long quotes set off from the rest of the text by indentation rather than quotation marks are generally introduced with a colon.

The first line of Lincoln's Gettysburg address is familiar to most Americans:

Fourscore and seven years ago our fathers brought forth on this continent a new nation, conceived in liberty and dedicated to the proposition that all men are created equal.

I quote from Shakespeare's *Sonnets*:

When I do count the clock that tells the time,
And see the brave day sunk in hideous night;
When I behold the violet past prime,
And sable curls all silver'd o'er with white . . .

It is also customary to begin a business letter with a colon.

Dear Senator Jordan:
To Whom It May Concern:
Gentlemen:
Dear Sir or Madam:

But in informal letters, use a comma.

Dear Mary,
Dear Father,

The colon is also used in introducing a list.

Please send the following:
1.   50 index cards,
2.   4 typewriter ribbons, and
3.   8 erasers.

Prepare the recipe as follows:
1. Slice the oranges thinly.
2. Arrange them in a circle around the strawberries.
3. Pour the liqueur over both fruits.

At least three ladies will have to be there to help:
1. Mrs. Goldman, who will greet the guests;
2. Harriet Sacher, who will serve the lunch; and
3. my sister, who will do whatever else needs to be done.

Finally, the colon is used between numbers when writing the time, between the volume and number or volume and page number of a journal, and also between the chapter and verse in the Bible.

4:30 P.M.
The Nation, 34:8
Genesis 5:18

The Semicolon

Semicolons (;) are sometimes called mild periods. They indicate a pause midway in length between the comma and the colon. Writing that contains many semicolons is usually in a dignified, formal style. To use them correctly, it is necessary to be able to recognize main clauses — complete ideas. **When two main clauses occur in a single sentence without a connecting word (*and, but, or, nor, for*), the appropriate mark of punctuation is the semicolon.**

It is not a good idea for you to leave the country right now; you should actually try to stay as long as you possibly can.
Music lightens life; literature deepens it.
In the past, boy babies were often dressed in blue; girls in pink. ("were often dressed" is understood in the second part of the sentence.)
Can't you see it's no good to go on alone; we'll starve to death if we keep traveling this way much longer.
Burgundy and maroon are very similar colors; scarlet is altogether different.

Notice how the use of the comma, period, and semicolon each gives a sentence a slightly different meaning.

Music lightens life; literature deepens it.
Just as music lightens life, literature deepens it.
Music lightens life. Literature deepens it.

The semicolon lends a certain balance to writing that would otherwise be difficult to achieve. Nonetheless, you should be careful not to overuse it. A comma can just as well join parts of a sentence with two main ideas; the semicolon is particularly appropriate if there is a striking contrast in the two ideas expressed.

> Ask not what your country can do for you; ask what you can do for your country.
>
> It started out as an ordinary day; it ended being the most extraordinary of her life.
>
> Our power to apprehend truth is limited; to seek it, limitless.

If any one of the following words or phrases are used to join together compound sentences, they are generally preceded by a semicolon:

then	however	thus	furthermore
hence	indeed	so	consequently
also	that is	yet	nevertheless
anyhow	in addition	in fact	on the other hand
likewise	moreover	still	meanwhile
instead	besides	otherwise	in other words
henceforth	for example	therefore	at the same time
even now			

> For a long time, people thought that women were inferior to men; *even now* it is not an easy attitude to overcome.
>
> Being clever and cynical, he succeeded in becoming president of the company; *meanwhile* his wife left him.
>
> Cigarette smoking has never interested me; *furthermore,* I couldn't care less if anyone else smokes or not.
>
> Some say Bach was the greatest composer of all time; *yet* he still managed to have an ordinary life in other ways: he and his wife had 20 children.
>
> We left wishing we could have stayed much longer; *in other words,* they showed us a good time.

When a series of complicated items are listed, or if there is internal punctuation in a series, the semicolon is sometimes used to make the meaning more clear.

> You can use your new car for many things: to drive to town or to the country; to impress your friends and neighbors; to protect yourself from rain on a trip away from home; and to borrow against should you need money right away.

> The scores from yesterday's games came in late last night: Pirates-6, Zoomers-3; Caterpillars-12, Steelys-8; Crashers-9, Links-8; and Greens-15, Uptowns-4.
>
> In October a bag of potatoes cost 69¢; in December 99¢; in February $1.09; in April $1.39. I wonder if this inflation will ever stop.

The semicolon is placed outside quotation marks or parentheses, unless it is part of the material enclosed in those marks.

> I used to call him "my lord and master"; it made him laugh every time.
>
> The weather was cold for that time of year (I was shivering wherever I went); nevertheless, we set out to hike to the top of that mountain.

Exercise: The Colon and Semicolon

> **DIRECTIONS:** Correctly place the colon and the semicolon in the following sentences.

1. I have only one thing to say don't do it.

2. They seemed compatible yet they did not get along.

3. She had only one goal in life to be a famous pianist.

4. He thought the problem was solved instead his solution proved to be entirely wrong.

5. By the end of the day there were only two things on her mind rest and relaxation.

Section 13: Quotation Marks

The proper use of quotation marks must be studied and learned, since some of their uses appear arbitrary and outside common sense.

The most common use of double quotation marks (" ") is to set off quoted words, phrases, and sentences.

> "If everybody minded their own business," said the Duchess in a hoarse growl, "the world would go round a great deal faster than it does."
>
> "Then you would say what you mean," the March Hare went on.

"I do," Alice hastily replied: "at least — at least I mean what I say — that's the same thing, you know."

"Not the same thing a bit!" said the Hatter. "Why, you might just as well say that 'I see what I eat' is the same thing as 'I eat what I see'!"

Both quotes from Lewis Carroll's *Alice in Wonderland*

In the last quote, single quotation marks are used to set off quoted material within a quote. Other examples of correct use of single quotation marks are:

"Shall I bring 'Rime of the Ancient Mariner' along with us?" she asked her brother.

Mrs. Green said, "The doctor told me, 'Go immediately to bed when you get home.'"

"If she said that to me," Katherine insisted, "I would tell her, 'I never intend to speak to you again! Goodbye, Susan.'"

Writing a Dialogue

When writing a dialogue, begin a new paragraph each time the speaker changes.

"Do you know what time it is?" asked Jane. "I don't want to be late for my class."

"Can't you see I'm busy?" snapped Mary. "Go into the kitchen if you want the time."

"It's easy to see you're in a bad mood today," replied Jane.

Use quotation marks to enclose words used as words (sometimes italics are used for this purpose).

"Judgment" had always been a difficult word for me to spell.

Do you know what "abstruse" means?

I always thought "nice" meant "particular" or "having exacting standards," but I know now it has acquired a much more general and vague meaning.

"Horse and buggy" and "bread and butter" can be used as either adjectives or nouns.

If slang is used within more formal writing, the slang words or phrases should be set off with quotation marks.

The "old boy" system is responsible for most promotions in today's corporate world.

I thought she was a "knockout," which made it difficult to relate to her as the supervisor.

Harrison's decision to "stick his neck out" by voicing dissent was applauded by the rest of the board members.

When words are meant to have an unusual or special significance to the reader—for instance, in displaying irony or humor—they are sometimes placed in quotation marks. This is, however, a practice to be avoided whenever possible. The reader should be able to get the intended meaning from the context.

For years, women were not allowed to buy real estate in order to "protect" them from unscrupulous dealers. (The writer is using somebody else's word; the use of the quotation marks shows he or she does not believe women needed protection.)

The "conversation" resulted in one black eye and a broken arm.

Our orders were always given as "suggestions."

To set off titles of radio and TV shows, poems, stories, and chapters in a book, use quotation marks. (Book, motion picture, newspaper, and magazine titles are underlined when written and italicized in text.)

The article "Moving South in the Southern Rain," by Jergen Smith in the *Southern News*, attracted the attention of our editor.

The assignment was "Childhood Development," chapter 18 of *Human Behavior*.

My favorite essay by Montaigne is "On Silence."

"I'm Gonna Wash that Man Right Out of My Hair" was the big hit song from *South Pacific*.

Whitman's "Song of the Open Road" may be the most famous poem from his *Leaves of Grass*.

"Seinfeld" led the TV ratings for years, didn't it?

Jackson Miller's "What's Your Opinion?" on WNYB stirs plenty of controversy every Thursday night.

"Jesu Joy of Man's Desiring" by J.S. Bach leaves you optimistic and glad to be alive.

I saw it in the "Guide" in the Sunday *Times*.

You will find Keats' "Ode on a Grecian Urn" in chapter 3, "The Romantic Era," in Lastly's *Selections from Great English Poets*.

Errors to Avoid

Be sure to remember that quotation marks always come in pairs. Do not make the mistake of using only one set.

NO: "You'll never convince me to move to the city, said Thurman. I consider it an insane asylum."

YES: "You'll never convince me to move to the city," said Thurman. "I consider it an insane asylum."

NO: "Idleness and pride tax with a heavier hand than kings and parliaments," Benjamin Franklin is supposed to have said. If we can get rid of the former, we may easily bear the latter."

YES: "Idleness and pride tax with a heavier hand than kings and parliaments," Benjamin Franklin is supposed to have said. "If we can get rid of the former, we may easily bear the latter."

When a quote consists of several sentences, do not put the quotation marks at the beginning and the end of each sentence; put them at the beginning and end of the entire quotation.

NO: "It was during his student days in Bonn that Beethoven fastened upon Schiller's poem." "The heady sense of liberation in the verses must have appealed to him." "They appealed to every German." — John Burke

YES: "It was during his student days in Bonn that Beethoven fastened upon Schiller's poem. The heady sense of liberation in the verses must have appealed to him. They appealed to every German." — John Burke

Instead of setting off a long quote with quotation marks, you may want to indent and single space it. If you do indent, do not use quotation marks.

> We are not enemies, but friends. We must not be enemies. Though passion may have strained, it must not break our bonds of affection. The mystic chords of memory, stre[t]ching from every battlefield, and patriot grave, to every living heart and hearthstone, all over this broad land, will yet swell the chorus of the Union, when again touched, as surely they will be, by the better angels of our nature.
> — Abraham Lincoln *First Inaugural Address*

Be careful not to use quotation marks with indirect quotation:

NO: Mary wondered "if she would ever get over it."

YES: Mary wondered if she would ever get over it.

NO: The nurse asked "how long it had been since we had visited the doctor's office."

YES: The nurse asked how long it had been since we had visited the doctor's office.

NO: "My exercise teacher told me," Mary said, "'that I should do these back exercises fifteen minutes each day.'"

YES: "My exercise teacher told me," Mary said, "that I should do these back exercises fifteen minutes each day."

When you quote several paragraphs, it is not sufficient to place quotation marks at the beginning and ending of the entire quote. Place quotation marks at the *beginning of each paragraph*, but only *at the end of the last paragraph*. Here is an abbreviated quotation for an example:

> "Here begins an odyssey through the world of classical mythology, starting with the creation of the world, proceeding to the divinities that once governed all aspects of human life. . . .
>
> "It is true that themes similar to the classical may be found in almost any corpus of mythology. . . . Even technology is not immune to the influence of Greece and Rome. . . .
>
> "We need hardly mention the extent to which painters and sculptors . . . have used and adapted classical mythology to illustrate the past, to reveal the human body, to express romantic or antiromantic ideals, or to symbolize any particular point of view."

Remember that commas and periods are always placed inside the quotation marks even if they are not actually part of the quote.

NO: "Life always gets colder near the summit", Nietzsche is purported to have said, "—the cold increases, responsibility grows".

YES: "Life always gets colder near the summit," Nietzsche is purported to have said, "—the cold increases, responsibility grows."

NO: "Get down here right away", John cried. "You'll miss the sunset if you don't".

YES: "Get down here right away," John cried. "You'll miss the sunset if you don't."

NO: "If my dog could talk", Mary mused, "I'll bet he would say, 'Take me for a walk right this minute'".

YES: "If my dog could talk," Mary mused, "I'll bet he would say, 'Take me for a walk right this minute.'"

Other marks of punctuation, such as question marks, exclamation points, colons and semicolons, go inside the quotation marks if they are part of the quoted material. If they are not part of the quote, however, they go outside the quotation mark. Be careful to distinguish between the guidelines for the comma and period, which always go inside the quotation marks, and those for the other marks of punctuation.

NO: "I'll always love you"! she exclaimed happily.

YES: "I'll always love you!" she exclaimed happily.

NO: Did you hear her say, "He'll be there early?"
(The question mark belongs to the entire sentence and not to the quote alone.)

YES: Did you hear her say, "He'll be there early"?

NO: She called down the stairs, "When are you coming"?
(The question mark belongs to the quote.)

YES: She called down the stairs, "When are you coming?"

NO: "Ask not what your country can do for you"; said Kennedy, "ask what you can do for your country:" a statement of genius, I think.
(The semicolon is part of the quoted material; the colon is not part of the quote, but belongs to the entire sentence.)

YES: "Ask not what your country can do for you;" said Kennedy, "ask what you can do for your country": a statement of genius, I think.

NO: "Let me out"! he cried. "Don't you have any pity"?

YES: "Let me out!" he cried. "Don't you have any pity?"

Remember to use only one mark of punctuation at the end of a sentence ending with a quotation.

NO: She thought out loud, "Will I ever finish this paper in time for that class?".

YES: She thought out loud, "Will I ever finish this paper in time for that class?"

NO: "Not the same thing a bit!", said the Hatter. "Why, you might just as well say that 'I see what I eat' is the same thing as 'I eat what I see'!".

YES: "Not the same thing a bit!" said the Hatter. "Why, you might just as well say that 'I see what I eat' is the same thing as 'I eat what I see'!"

Exercise: Quotation Marks

DIRECTIONS: Correctly punctuate the following sentences.

1. Take an umbrella, said his mother, it looks like rain.

2. I haven't seen my old lady in five years, he exclaimed.

3. Can I write a comparative essay using To Autumn and Ode to a Nightingale for the assignment, asked the student.

4. My Favorite Things is a popular song from The Sound of Music, he remarked.

5. Do you understand the difference between overt and covert?

6. The washing machine went haywire this afternoon.

7. They wondered if they could do the job.

8. "Joseph locked the door"; said Andy "then, he put the key under the doormat".

9. You and Your Health is a popular show on WMCA.

10. Mary said "She is leaving for California tomorrow"!

11. "Don't ask any questions now", Susan exclaimed, "I'm trying to read".

12. "I can't believe it"! she exclaimed.

Section 14: The Apostrophe

Use the apostrophe to form contractions: to indicate that letters or figures have been omitted.

can't (cannot)	o'clock (of the clock)
I'll (I will)	it's (it is)
memories of '42 (1942)	won't (will not)
you've (you have)	they're (they are)

Notice that the apostrophe is *always* placed where a letter or letters have been omitted. Avoid such careless errors as writing *wo'nt* instead of *won't*, for example. Contractions are generally not used in formal writing. They are found primarily in speech and informal writing.

An apostrophe is also used to indicate the plural form of letters, figures, and words that normally don't take a plural form. In such cases it would be confusing to add only an "s."

He quickly learned his *r*'s and *s*'s.

Children have difficulties in remembering to dot their *i*'s and cross their *t*'s.

Most of the *Ph.D.*'s and *M.D.*'s understand the new technology they are using for anticancer drugs.

Her *2*'s always looked like her *4*'s.

Marion used too many *the*'s and *and*'s in her last paper for English literature.

Whenever possible, try to form plurals of numbers and of single or multiple letters used as words by adding only "s."

the ABCs	the 1940s
in threes and fours	three Rs

Placement of the Apostrophe to Indicate Possession

In spoken English, the same pronunciation is used for the plural, singular, possessive, and plural possessive of most nouns. It is only by the context that the listener is able to tell the difference in the words used by the speaker. In written English, the spelling as well as the context tells the reader the meaning of the noun the writer is using. The writer has only to master the placement of the apostrophe so that the meaning is clearly conveyed to the reader. These words are pronounced alike but have different meanings:

Plural	Singular Possessive	Plural Possessive
neighbors	neighbor's	neighbors'
doctors	doctor's	doctors'
weeks	week's	weeks'
sopranos	soprano's	sopranos'
civilizations	civilization's	civilizations'

If you aren't sure of the apostrophe's placement, you can determine it accurately by this simple test: change the possessive phrase into "belonging to" or an "of" phrase to discover the basic noun. You will find this a particularly useful trick for some of the more confusing possessive forms such as those on words that end in "s" or "es."

Keats' poem: The poem belonging to Keats. The base noun is *Keats*; the possessive is Keats' or Keats's, not Keat's or Keats'es.

The Joneses' house: The house of the Joneses (plural of Jones). Base is *Joneses*; possessive is Joneses', not Jones' or Jones'es.

Four months' pay: The pay of four months. *Months* is the base noun; the possessive is months', not month's.

In two hours' time: In the time of two hours. *Hours* is the base noun; the possessive is hours', not hour's.

The lioness' strength: The strength of the lioness. *Lioness* is the base noun; the possessive is lioness' or lioness's, not lioness'es or liones's.

It is anybody's guess: The guess of anybody. *Anybody* is the base noun; the possessive is anybody's, not anybodys' or anybodies'.

Exercise: The Apostrophe

Contractions

> **DIRECTIONS:** Write the contractions of the following.

1. she will, _____

2. shall not, _____

3. Class of 1981, _____

4. does not, _____

5. they have, _____

6. We are, _____

7. This boat isnt yours. We sold our's last year to Roberts parents.

8. At 10 oclock theyll meet us at Macys department store.

Possession

1. lady, _____, _____

2. child, _____, _____

3. cashier, _____, _____

4. Filipino, _____, _____

5. country, _____, _____

Section 15: Stops

There are three ways to end a sentence:

1. a period

2. a question mark

3. an exclamation point

The Period

Periods end all sentences that are not questions or exclamations. In speech, the end of a sentence is indicated with a full pause. The period is the counterpart of this pause in writing.

> Go get me my paper. I'm anxious to see the news.
> Into each life some rain must fall. Last night some fell into mine.
> The moon is round. The stars look small.
> Mary and Janet welcomed the newcomer. She was noticeably happy.

When a question is intended as a suggestion and the listener is not expected to answer, or when a question is asked indirectly as part of a sentence, a period is also used.

Mimi wondered if the parade would ever end.
May we hear from you soon?
Will you please send the flowers you advertised?
We'll never know who the culprit was.

Periods also follow most abbreviations and contractions.

N.Y.	Dr.	Jr.	Sr.
etc.	Jan.	Mrs.	Mr.
Esq.	cont.	A.M.	A.D.

Periods (or parentheses) are also used after a letter or number in a series.

a. apples	1. president
b. oranges	2. vice president
c. pears	3. secretary

Errors to Avoid

Be sure to omit the period after a quotation mark preceded by a period. Only one stop is necessary to end a sentence.

She said, "Hold my hand." (no period after the end quotes)
"Don't go into the park until later."
"It's not my fault," he said. "She would have taken the car anyway."

After many abbreviations, particularly for organizations or agencies, no period is used (check your dictionary if in doubt).

AFL-CIO	NAACP	GM
FBI	NATO	IBM
TV	UN	HEW

The Question Mark

Use a question mark to end a direct question even if it is not in the form of a question. The question mark in writing is the same as the rising tone of voice used to indicate a question in speech. If you read the following two sentences aloud, you will see the difference in tone between a statement and a question composed of the same words.

Mary is here.
Mary is here?

Here are some more examples of correct use of question marks; pay special attention to the way they are used with other punctuation:

Where will we go next?
Would you like coffee or tea?
"Won't you," he asked, "please lend me a hand?"
"Will they ever give us our freedom?" the prisoner asked.
"To be or not to be?" was the question asked by Hamlet.
Who asked "When?"

Question marks indicate a full stop and lend a different emphasis to a sentence than do commas. Compare these pairs of sentences:

Was the sonata by Beethoven? or Brahms? or Chopin?
Was the sonata by Beethoven, or Brahms, or Chopin?

Did they walk to the park? climb the small hill? take the bus to town? or go skating out back?
Did they walk to the park, climb the small hill, take the bus to town, or go skating out back?

Sometimes question marks are placed in parentheses. This indicates doubt or uncertainty about the facts being reported:

The bombing started at 3:00 A.M.(?)
She said the dress cost 200,000 (?) dollars.
Harriet Stacher [18(?)-1914] was well thought of in her time.
Hippocrates [460(?)-(?)377 B.C.] is said to be the father of modern medicine.

The Exclamation Point

An exclamation point ends an emphatic statement. It should be used only to express strong emotions such as surprise, disbelief, or admiration. If it is used too often for mild expressions of emotion, it loses its effectiveness.

Let go of me!
Help! Fire!
It was a wonderful day!
What a beautiful woman she is!
Who shouted "Fire!" (notice no question mark is necessary)
Fantastic!
"Unbelievable!" she gasped. (notice no comma is necessary)
"You'll never win!" he cried.
Where else can I go! (The use of the exclamation point shows that this is a strong statement even though it is worded like a question.)

Avoid Overuse

The following is an example of the overuse of exclamation points:

Dear Susan,

I was so glad to see you last week! You looked better than ever! Our talk meant so much to me! I can hardly wait until we get together again! Could you believe how long it has been! Let's never let that happen again! Please write as soon as you get the chance! I can hardly wait to hear from you!

Your friend,
Nora

Exercise: Stops

> **DIRECTIONS:** In the following sentences correctly supply periods, question marks, and exclamation points.

1. "Good gracious" she said "Didn't you know that I was coming"

2. Mr. Morgan works for the CIA

3. Alexander wondered if it was time to go

4. Leave me alone Can't you see that I'm busy

5. "How many boxes did you buy" asked Dr. Jones

Section 16: Interjections, Dashes, and Parentheses

Interjections

An interjection is a word or group of words used as an exclamation to express emotion. It need not be followed by an exclamation point. Often an interjection is followed by a comma (see Section 11: The Comma) if it is not very intense. Technically, the interjection has no grammatical relation to other words in the sentence, yet it is still considered a part of speech.

Examples:

Oh dear, I forgot my keys again.
Ah! Now do you understand?
Ouch! I didn't realize that the stove was hot.
Oh, excuse me. I didn't realize that you were next on line.

Dashes

Use the dash to indicate a sudden or unexpected break in the normal flow of the sentence. It can also be used in the place of parentheses or of commas if the meaning is clarified. Usually the dash gives the material it sets off special emphasis. (On a typewriter, two hyphens (--) indicate a dash.)

> Could you — I hate to ask! — help me with these boxes?
> When we left town — a day never to be forgotten — they had a record snowfall.
> She said — we all heard it — "The safe is not locked."
> These are the three ladies — Mrs. Jackson, Miss Harris, and Ms. Forrester — you hoped to meet last week.
> The sight of the Andromeda Galaxy — especially when seen for the first time — is astounding.
> That day was the longest in her life — or so it seemed to her.

A dash is often used to summarize a series of ideas that have already been expressed.

> Freedom of speech, freedom to vote, and freedom of assembly — these are the cornerstones of democracy.
> Carbohydrates, fats, and proteins — these are the basic kinds of food we need.
> Jones, who first suggested we go; Marshall, who made all the arrangements; and Kline, who finally took us there — these were the three men I admired most for their courage.
> James, Howard, Marianne, Angela, Catherine — all were displeased with the decision of the teacher.

The dash is also used to note the author of a quotation that is set off in the text.

> Nothing is good or bad but thinking makes it so.
> > — William Shakespeare
> Under every grief and pine
> Runs a joy with silken twine.
> > — William Blake

Parentheses

To set off material that is only loosely connected to the central meaning of the sentence, use parentheses [( )].

Most men (at least most that I know) like wine, women, and song, but have too much work and not enough time for such enjoyments.

On Tuesday evenings and Thursday afternoons (the times I don't have classes), the television programs are not too exciting.

Last year at Vale (we go there every year), the skiing was the best I've ever seen.

In New York (I've lived there all my life and ought to know), you have to have a license for a gun.

What must be done to think clearly and calmly (is it even possible?) and then make the decision?

Watch out for other punctuation when you use parentheses. Punctuation that refers to the material enclosed in the parentheses occurs inside the marks. Punctuation belonging to the rest of the sentence comes outside the parentheses.

I thought I knew the poem by heart (boy, was I wrong!).

For a long time (too long as far as I'm concerned), women were thought to be inferior to men.

We must always strive to tell the truth. (Are we even sure we know what truth is?)

When I first saw a rose (don't you think it's the most beautiful flower?), I thought it must be man-made.

Exercise: Interjections, Dashes, and Parentheses

Interjections and Dashes

> **DIRECTIONS:** Read the following sentences. What effect does the dash have on the writing, especially the tone and mood?

1. Can you? — I would be ever so grateful — I'm having so much difficulty.

2. Could it be — no it can't be — not after all these years.

3. Time and patience — two simple words — yet why are they so hard for me to remember?

4. Most of the paintings in the gallery — in fact all but one — were done in the nineteenth century.

5. According to John Locke, these are man's inalienable rights — life, liberty, and property.

Parentheses

> **DIRECTIONS:** Read the following sentences. What effect does the use of parentheses have on the writing? Also, make any necessary corrections.

1. The choice (in my opinion,) was a good one.

2. Linda's comment ("Where did you get that dress")? wasn't intended to be sarcastic.

3. After today (and what a day it was!) I will begin to work harder.

4. Last summer in Cape Cod (this was the first year we went there,) we did a lot of sightseeing.

5. The first time I went driving (do you remember the day)?, I was so scared.

Section 17: Capitalization

When a letter is capitalized, it calls special attention to itself. This attention should be for a good reason. There are standard uses for capital letters as well as much difference of opinion as to what should and should not be capitalized. In general, capitalize 1) all proper nouns, 2) the first word of a sentence, and 3) a direct quotation.

Names of Ships, Aircrafts, Spacecraft, and Trains

(Abbreviations preceding names and designations of class or make are not italicized.)

Apollo 13	*Mariner IV*
DC-10	S.S. *United States*
Sputnik II	Boeing 767

Names of Deities

God	Jupiter
Allah	Holy Ghost
Buddha	Diana
Jehovah	Shiva

Geological Periods

Neolithic age	Cenozoic era
late Pleistocene times	Age of Reptiles
Ice Age	Tertiary period

Names of Astronomical Bodies

Venus	Big Dipper
the Milky Way	Halley's comet
Ursa Major	North Star
Scorpio	Deneb
the Crab nebula	Pleiades

(Note that sun, moon, and earth are not capitalized unless they are used with other astronomical terms that are capitalized.)

Personifications

Reliable *Nature* brought her promise of Spring.

Bring on *Melancholy* in his sad might.

Morning in the bowl of night has flung the stone that set the stars to flight.

Historical Periods

the Middle Ages	World War I
Reign of Terror	Great Depression
Christian Era	Roaring Twenties
Age of Louis XIV	Renaissance

Organizations, Associations, and Institutions

Girl Scouts of America	North Atlantic Treaty Organization
Young Men's Christian Association	Kiwanis Club
the Trenton Thunder	League of Women Voters
Unitarian Church	Common Market
New Jersey Transit	New Jersey Symphony Orchestra
Rancocas Valley Regional High School	the Jaycees

Government and Judicial Entities

United States Court of Appeals	Committee on Foreign Affairs
Camden City Council	House of Commons

Senate	Parliament
Arkansas Supreme Court	House of Representatives
Peace Corps	Department of State
Municipal Court of Chicago	Newton Board of Education
Census Bureau	the Library of Congress

A general term that accompanies a specific name is capitalized only if it follows the specific name. If it stands alone or comes before the specific name, it is put in lowercase. This rule does *not* apply, however, when the general term directly precedes a person's name, thus acting as part of their title.

Washington State	the state of Washington
Central Park	the park
Golden Gate Bridge	the bridge
Tropic of Capricorn	the tropics
Glen Brook High School	the high school in Glen Brook
Monroe Doctrine	the doctrine originated by Monroe
the Milky Way Galaxy	our galaxy, the Milky Way
the Musconetcong River	the river
Easter Day	the day we celebrate Easter
Treaty of Versailles	the treaty signed at Versailles
Webster's Dictionary	a dictionary by Webster
Senator Dixon	the senator from Illinois
President Andrew Jackson	the president of the U.S.
Pope John XXIII	the pope
Queen Elizabeth I	the queen, Elizabeth I

Use a capital to start a sentence or a sentence fragment.

Our car would not start.
When will you leave? I need to know right away.
Never!
Let me in! Right now!

When a sentence appears within a sentence, start it with a capital.

The main question is, Where do we start?
We had only one concern: When would we eat?
My sister said, "I'll find the Monopoly set."
He answered, "We can only stay a few minutes."

In poetry, it is usual practice to capitalize the first word of each line even if the word comes in the middle of a sentence.

When I consider everything that grows
Holds in perfection but a little moment,
That this huge stage produceth naught but shows,
Whereon the stars in secret influence comment.

— William Shakespeare

She dwells with Beauty — Beauty that must die;
And Joy, whose hand is ever at his lips
Bidding Adieu.

— John Keats

The most important words of titles are capitalized. Those words not capitalized are conjunctions (e.g., *and, or, but*), articles (e.g., *a, the, an*), and short prepositions (e.g., *of, on, by, for*). The first and last words of a title must always be capitalized.

A Man for All Seasons	*Crime and Punishment*
Of Mice and Men	"Let Me In"
Rise of the West	"What to Look For"
"Sonata in G-Minor"	"The Ever-Expanding West"
Strange Life of Ivan Osokin	"Rubaiyat of Omar Khayyam"
"All in the Family"	*Symphony No. 41*
"Ode to Billy Joe"	"Piano Concerto No. 5"

Exercise: Capitalization

> **DIRECTIONS:** The following sentences contain errors in capitalization. Correct these sentences by making words capital where necessary and other words lowercase where necessary.

1. Where is the crab Nebula?

2. The girl scouts of America sells delicious cookies.

3. This year, senator Burns will run for reelection.

4. Barbara said, "let me know when you are off the phone."

5. beth's new car is a black dodge daytona, which she purchased at the dodge dealer in new york city.

6. mike and jackie are both graduates of edison high school.

7. glaciers from the ice age still exist.

Now that you have brushed up on the skills needed to succeed on Language Arts questions, you should take the following exercise. This exercise is in the form of multiple-choice questions and will help you become accustomed to dealing with these types of questions.

Exercise: Writing Skills

The following passage is written in the form of a popular magazine. Read the text and answer the questions.

[1]The Lincoln Cent was first struck in 1909 to celebrate the hundredth anniversary of the birth of Abraham Lincoln, our sixteenth president. [2]Designed by Victor D. Brenner, the coin carried the motto "In God We Trust" — the first time it appeared on this denomination coin. [3]It is interesting that the law for the motto was passed during Lincoln's administration as president. [4]Though we might not think so at first glance, the lowly Cent is a fitting memorial for the great man whose profile graces this most common coin of the realm, and a tolerable symbol for the nation whose commerce it serves.

[5]The obverse has the profile of Lincoln as he looked during the trying years of the War Between the States. [6]Faced with the immense problems of a divided nation, the prevention of the split between North and South was difficult. [7]"A house divided against itself cannot stand," he warned the nation. [8]With the outbreak of war at Fort Sumter. Lincoln was saddened to see his beloved country caught up in the senseless war in which father fought against son, brother against brother. [9]Throughout America, war captured the attention of people: the woman who saved the lives of the wounded, the soldier waiting to go into battle, the bewildered child trying hard to understand the sound of guns. [10]Lincoln stood on the broad, silent battlefield at Gettysburg in 1863 to dedicate the site as a national cemetery. [11]Gettysburg had been the scene of some of the most bitter fighting of the war and had ended in a Union victory.
[12] _____

_____.

[13]In his special address at Gettysburg, he called upon the American people to end the war. [14]His words boomed out over the large audience before him:

[15]. . . It is rather for us [the living] to be here dedicated to the great task remaining before us — that from these honored dead we take increased devotion to that cause for which they gave the last full measure of devotion; that we here highly resolve that these dead shall not have died in

vain; that this nation under God, shall have a new birth of freedom; and that government of the people, by the people and for the people, shall not perish from the earth."

[16]Barely a month before the end of the war, Lincoln took the oath of office a secondly time as president. [17]With the war still raging, his inaugural address took on added meaning:

. . . With malice toward none, with charity for all, with firmness in the right as God gives us to see the right, let us strive on to finish the work we are in, to bind up the nation's wounds, to care for him who shall have borne the battle and for his widow and his orphan, to do all which may achieve and cherish a just and lasting peace among ourselves and with all nations.

1.   Which of the following sentences, used in place of the blank lines labeled Part 12, would best fit the writer's purpose and be consistent with the point in the paragraph?

   (A) Lincoln felt the victory was pyrrhic and worthless.

   (B) The president was elated over the victory and felt that this was an opportunity to encourage more young men to join the Union ranks.

   (C) Lincoln was pleased with the victory but deeply concerned over the deaths of so many soldiers.

   (D) Lincoln, depressed over the loss of so many young men in the Union, wanted to use the dedication speech to whip up hatred for the Confederate cause.

2.   Which of the following changes is needed in the third paragraph?

   (A) Part 16: Change "end" to "climax."

   (B) Part 16: Change "secondly" to "second."

   (C) Part 17: Change "With" to "Of."

   (D) Part 17: Change "on" to "in."

3.   Which of the following changes is needed in the second paragraph?

   (A) Part 5: Change "has" to "had."

   (B) Part 6: Change "the prevention of the split between North and South was difficult" to "Lincoln found it difficult to prevent the split between North and South."

(C) Part 9: Change "waiting" to "waited."

(D) Part 10: Change "site" to "sight."

4.   Which of the following parts is a nonstandard sentence?

(A) Part 2   (C) Part 8

(B) Part 4   (D) Part 11

The following passage is written in the form of an educational textbook. Read the text and answer the questions.

[1]Dr. Robert Goddard at one time a physics professor at Clark University, Worcester, Massachusetts was largely responsible for the sudden interest in rockets back in the twenties. [2]When Dr. Goddard first started his experiments with rockets, no related technical information was available. [3]He started a new science, industry, and field of engineering. [4]Through his scientific experiments, he pointed the way to the development of rockets as we know them today. [5]The Smithsonian Institute agreed to finance his experiments in 1920. [6]From these experiments he wrote a paper titled "A Method of Reaching Extreme Altitudes," in which he outlined a space rocket of the step (multistage) principle, theoretically capable of reaching the moon.

[7]Goddard discovered that with a properly shaped, smooth, tapered nozzle he could increase the ejection velocity eight times with the same weight of fuel. [8]This would not only drive a rocket eight times faster, but sixty-four times farther, according to his theory. [9]Early in his experiments he found that solid-fuel rockets would not give him the high power or the duration of power needed for a dependable supersonic motor capable of extreme altitudes. [10]_____.

[11]It attained an altitude of 184 feet and a speed of 60 m.p.h. [12]This seems small as compared to present-day speeds and heights of missile flights, but instead of trying to achieve speed or altitude at this time, Dr. Goddard was trying to develop a dependable rocket motor.

[13]Dr. Goddard later was the first to fire a rocket that reached a speed faster than the speed of sound. [14]He was first to develop a gyroscopic steering <u>thing</u> for rockets. [15]The first to use vanes in the jet stream for rocket stabilization during <u>the initial phase</u> of a rocket flight. [16]And he was first to patent the idea of step rockets. [17]After proving on paper and in <u>actual</u> tests that a rocket can travel in a vacuum, he developed the mathematical theory of rocket propulsion and rocket flight, including basic

designs for long-range rockets. [18]All of his information was available to military men before World War II, but evidently its immediate use did not seem applicable.

[19]Near the end of World War II we started intense <u>work</u> on rocket-powered guided missiles, using the experiments and developments of Dr. Goddard and the American Rocket Society.

5. Which of the following sentences, used in place of the blank line labeled Part 10, would best fit the writer's pattern of development in the second paragraph?

   (A) Consequently, Doctor Goddard was able to fire a rocket successfully.

   (B) On the other hand, Dr. Goddard fired a rocket successfully.

   (C) On 16 March 1926, after many trials, Dr. Goddard successfully fired, for the first time in history, a liquid-fuel rocket into the air.

   (D) Firing a rocket successfully was thus an enormous difficulty.

6. Which of the following should be changed to reflect correct punctuation in the first paragraph?

   (A) Part 1: Put commas in after "Goddard" and after "Massachusetts."

   (B) Part 2: Remove the comma after "rockets."

   (C) Part 4: Put a comma in after "rockets."

   (D) Part 6: Remove the comma after "principle."

7. Which of the following parts of the third paragraph is a nonstandard sentence?

   (A) Part 14   (C) Part 16

   (B) Part 15   (D) Part 17

8. Which of the underlined words in the third or fourth paragraph should be replaced by more precise or appropriate words?

   (A) thing   (C) actual

   (B) the initial phase   (D) work

The following passage is written in the form of a feature editorial. Read the text and answer the questions.

[1]We've grown accustomed to seeing this working woman hanging from the subway strap during commuting hours. [2]We may refer disparagingly to her tailored suit and little tie but we no longer visualize her in a house dress with her hair uncombed. [3]The woman who leaves her children to go to work in the morning is no longer a pariah in her community or her family. [4]Her paycheck is more than pin money; it buys essential family staples and often supports the entire family. [5]_____ _____.

[6]The situation for men has also changed as a result of women's massive entry into the work force for the better. [7]Men who would once have felt unrelenting pressure to remain with one firm and climb the career ladder are often freed up by a second income to change careers in midlife. [8]They enjoy greatest intimacy and involvement with their children.

[9]The benefits for business are also readily apparent. [10]No senior manager in the country would deny that the huge generation of women who entered management seven or eight years ago has functioned superbly, often outperforming men.

[11]Yet the prevailing message from the media on the subject of women and business is one filled with pessimism. [12]We hear about women leaving their employers in the lurch when they go on maternity leave. [13]Or we hear the flip side, that women are overly committed to their careers and neglectful of their families. [14]And in fact, it is true that problems arising from women's new work force role do exist, side by side with the benefits.

[15]The problems hurt business as well as individuals and their families, affordable quality childcare, for one example, is still a distant dream. [16]Some women are distracted at work, and men who would have felt secure about their children when their wives were home are also anxious and distracted. [17]Distraction also impedes the productivity of some high-achieving women with the birth of their first child and causes some to depart with the birth of their second.

9. **Which of the following sentences, if added in the blank lines for Part 5, would be most consistent with the writer's point, purpose, and audience?**

   (A) The working woman is a rare and unexpected phenomenon.

   (B) The presence of women in the management ranks of corporations is a reality.

   (C) Women in business are the outcasts of the working world.

   (D) Taking the career woman seriously is like worrying about one more drop of rainwater in a barrelful.

10. Which of the following parts of the passage displays a nonstandard placement of a modifying phrase?

   (A) Part 1   (C) Part 6

   (B) Part 3   (D) Part 7

11. Which of the following parts of the passage displays a nonstandard use of a comparative form?

   (A) Part 4   (C) Part 10

   (B) Part 8   (D) Part 13

12. Which of the following parts of the passage is a nonstandard sentence?

   (A) Part 14   (C) Part 16

   (B) Part 15   (D) Part 17

The following passage is written in the form of a student essay. Read the text and answer the questions.

[1]In the past forty years, television has become a very popular past time for almost everyone. [2]From the time the mother places the baby in her jumpseat in front of the television as she is drinking orange juice until the time the senior citizen in the retirement home watches Vanna White turn the letters on "Wheel of Fortune," Americans spend endless hours in front of the "boob tube." [3]_____

_____.

[4]When my mother was a little girl, what did children do to entertain themselves? [5]They played. [6]Their games usually involved social interaction with other children as well as imaginatively creating entertainment for themselves. [7]They also developed hobbies like woodworking and sewing. [8]Today, few children really know how to play with each other or entertain themselves. [9]Instead, they sit in front of the television, glued to cartoons that are senseless and often violent. [10]Even if they watch educational programs like "Sesame Street," they don't really have to do anything but watch and listen to what the answer to the question is.

[11]Teenagers, also, use television as a way of avoiding doing things that will be helping them mature. [12]How many kids does much homework anymore? [13]Why not? [14]Because they work part-time jobs and come home from work tired and relax in front of the television.

13. Which of the following sentences, if added in the blank lines allowed for Part 3, would best reflect the writer's point of view?

    (A) However, television is unimaginative as a form of entertainment.

    (B) Television takes up too much time in our daily lives.

    (C) I believe that television can become an addiction that provides an escape from the problems of the world and from facing responsibility for your own life.

    (D) Television is a demanding as well as educational national pastime.

14. Which of the following sentences uses a nonstandard verb form?

    (A) Part 4   (C) Part 8

    (B) Part 7   (D) Part 12

15. Which of the following sentences in the passage is nonstandard?

    (A) Part 2   (C) Part 10

    (B) Part 7   (D) Part 14

16. Which of the following changes is needed in the first paragraph?

    (A) Part 1: Change "has become" to "is."

    (B) Part 2: Change "she" to "the mother" or "the baby."

    (C) Part 2: Change "watches" to "watched."

    (D) Part 4: Change "When" to "Being that."

WRITING EXERCISES

ANSWER KEY

Exercise – Sentence Fragments/Run-on Sentences

1. Fragment: We went out after the rain stopped.

2. Run-on: Mow the lawn. It is much too long.

3. Run-on: The settlement you reached seems fair.

4. Fragment: My eyes get tired when I read, especially at night.

5. Run-on: It was impossible to get through on the phone, since the lines were down because of the storm.

Exercise – Short Sentences/Wordiness

1. He graduated from college and, in no time, found a job and rented an apartment. He was happy.

2. The book she lent me was lengthy, boring, and unenjoyable. I wouldn't recommend it to anyone.

3. We have nothing to do because our plans to go on a picnic have been ruined by the rain.

4. She immediately obliged anyone who telephoned for help with their homework.

5. She liked to paint and was quite good; unfortunately, materials are expensive and she cannot afford them.

Exercise – Misplaced Modifiers

1. I saw a stray dog while I was riding the bus this afternoon.

2. The clothing was given in large packages to the poor.

3. I found five dollars while I was eating lunch in the park.

4. While we were in our car, we saw two girls riding bicycles.

5. When the car crashed, I jumped up from quietly reading my book.

Exercise – Parallel Structure

1. In the summer I usually like to swim and water-ski.

2. The professor explained the cause, the effect, and the results.

3. Mary read the book, studied the examples, and took the test.

4. Mark watched how John started the car, and how he left the curb.

5. They bought the house because of its location and its affordability.

Exercise – Phrases

1. "to solve the crime": (I); "to maintain justice": (I)

2. "on the billboard" (PR); "billboard" (OP)

3. "having painted the house" (P)

4. "Staying in shape" (G)

5. "with pure logic" (PR); "logic" (OP)

Exercise – Clauses

1. Phrase

2. Clause

3. Phrase

4. Clause

5. Clause

Exercise – Subject-Verb Agreement

1. Either her mother or her father usually drives her to school on rainy days.

2. There are, if I calculated right, two hundred dollars left in my bank account.

3. Mary and her friends were late for the test.

4. Economics is a major taught in many colleges.

5. The first years of high school are the most difficult.

Exercise – Comparison of Adjectives

1. He was *saddest* to leave. (adjective)

2. She ran *faster* than the others on the team. (adverb)

3. Throughout school, they were *the best* in math. (adjective)

4. This class is *more interesting* than European history class. (adjective)

5. He arrived *sooner* than I did. (adverb)

Exercise – Pronouns

A. Relative Pronouns

1. who
2. what
3. which
4. whichever
5. whatever

B. Relative Pronouns

1. whom
2. whom
3. who
4. who
5. who

C. Interrogative and Demonstrative Pronouns

Interrogatives

1. We wondered *who* would come to the party.

2. I asked Janet *what* she wanted to do tonight.

3. I had no idea *which* club she wanted to go to.

4. I said we would go to *whichever* one she wanted to.

5. I have fun with Janet *whatever* we do.

Demonstratives

1. *Those* are the red shoes I want.

2. I was too nervous to speak to *that* girl.

3. He was *so* sick after his first gin and tonic that he never drank another.

4. It was *such* an exciting party.

5. I must buy her *that* watch.

D. Reflexive Pronouns

1. ourselves (object, refers to "we")

2. myself (object, refers to "I")

3. yourself (object, refers to "you" understood)

4. itself (object, refers to "play")

5. themselves (object, refers to "they")

E. Reflexive Pronouns

1. Both James and they went to the beach.

2. Jack himself read the speech.

3. I will unload the car.

4. They finished the painting themselves.

5. He mowed the lawn himself.

F. Personal Pronouns

1. I

2. him

3. We

4. I

5. she

6. he

7. they

8. they

9. we

10. she

11. I

12. her and me

13. he

14. us

G. Possessive Pronouns

1. whose

2. her

3. that

4. His

5. mine

H. Expletives

1. It's
2. There
3. It's

4. It
5. It's

I. Pronouns

1. her
2. their
3. its

4. their
5. his

Exercise – Conjunctions

1. John's best assets are his personality and his swimming ability.

2. I heard on the radio that the play is closing this week.

3. I was reading the paper when the phone rang.

4. Susan often ate vegetables but not fruits.

5. Please send me either an answer to the questions or opinions on the project.

Exercise – The Comma

1. However, I am willing to reconsider.

   Reason: "However" is a transitional word and requires a comma after it.

2. She descended the long, winding staircase.

   Reason: A comma is used in a series to emphasize each adjective.

3. Whenever I practice my violin, my family closes the windows.

   Reason: Use a comma after a long introductory phrase.

4. While driving, Francis never took his eyes off the road.

   Reason: When the introductory phrase includes a "verbal," a comma is necessary.

5. The car, which I bought last year, is in the garage.

   Reason: The modifying group of words ("which I bought last year") is not vital to the meaning of the sentence and, therefore, is set off by commas.

6. "Answer the door," his mother said loudly.

   Reason: Use a comma to set off direct quotations.

7. Miss, can I ask you for the time?

   Reason: Use a comma to set off direct address.

8. He was, after all, an ex-convict.

   Reason: Use commas to set off parenthetical words and phrases.

9. I'm so bored, aren't you?

   Reason: Use a comma to set off tag questions.

10. The old, tall, shady tree is wonderful during the summer.

    Reason: When an adjective series describes a noun, use a comma to separate and emphasize each adjective.

11. George, Gary, and Bill were on line early this morning. They bought their tickets, read the newspaper, and spoke for a while.

    Reason: For both sentences use a comma to separate words, phrases, and whole ideas (clauses).

12. The author, James Grey, was awarded the prize.

    Reason: Use commas to set off nonrestrictive words.

13. She attended school in London, England, last year.

    Reason: Use commas to set off geographical names.

14. No correction necessary.

15. His weight, not his height, prevented him from competing in the race.

    Reason: Use commas to set off contrasting elements.

Exercise – The Colon and Semicolon

1. I have only one thing to say: don't do it.

2. They seemed compatible; yet they did not get along.

3. She had only one goal in life: to be a famous pianist.

4. He thought the problem was solved; instead, his solution proved to be entirely wrong.

5. By the end of the day there were only two things on her mind: rest and relaxation.

Exercise – Quotation Marks

1. "Take an umbrella," said his mother: "It looks like rain."

2. "I haven't seen my 'old lady' in five years!" he exclaimed.

3. "Can I write a comparative essay using 'To Autumn' and 'Ode to a Nightingale' for the assignment?" asked the student.

4. "'My Favorite Things' is a popular song from *The Sound of Music,*" he remarked.

5. Do you understand the difference between "overt" and "covert"?

6. The washing machine went "haywire" this afternoon.

7. They wondered if they could do the job.

8. "Joseph locked the door," said Andy; "then, he put the key under the doormat."

9. "You and Your Health" is a popular show on WMCA.

10. Mary said, "She is leaving for California tomorrow!"

11. "Don't ask any questions now!" Susan exclaimed. "I'm trying to read."

12. "I can't believe it!" she exclaimed.

Exercise – The Apostrophe

Contractions

1. she'll

2. won't

3. Class of '81

4. doesn't

5. they've

6. We're

7. This boat isn't yours. We sold ours last year to Robert's parents.

8. At 10 o'clock they'll meet us at Macy's department store.

Possession

1. lady's, ladies'

2. child's, children's

3. cashier's, cashiers'

4. Filipino's, Filipinos'

5. country's, countries'

Exercise – Stops

1. "Good gracious!" she said. "Didn't you know that I was coming?"

2. Mr. Morgan works for the CIA.

3. Alexander wondered if it was time to go.

4. Leave me alone! Can't you see that I'm busy?

5. "How many boxes did you buy?" asked Dr. Jones.

Exercise – Interjections, Dashes, and Parentheses

Interjections and Dashes

1. The use of the dash makes the sentence more urgent.

2. The use of the dash helps to convey a feeling of disbelief.

3. The words set off by dashes emphasize and modify the key words, "Time and patience."

4. The dashes help to emphasize and clarify the subject.

5. The dash is used to set off specifics.

Parentheses

1. The choice (in my opinion) was a good one. The comma in the sentence is unnecessary. Alternatively: The choice, in my opinion, was a good one. The parentheses are unnecessary in the sentence. "In my opinion" is not very necessary, since the statements made in writing are usually considered to be the author's, unless otherwise indicated.

2. Linda's comment ("Where did you get that dress?") wasn't intended to be sarcastic. The parentheses are a clear, effective method for containing a quote.

3. The parentheses properly set off material that is loosely connected to the central meaning of the sentence.

4. Last summer in Cape Cod (that was the first year we went there) we did a lot of sightseeing. The parentheses effectively contain the additional information.

5. The first time I went driving (do you remember the day?) I was so scared. The parentheses smoothly incorporate an important aside from the speaker.

Exercise – Capitalization

1. Where is the Crab nebula?

2. The Girl Scouts of America sells delicious cookies.

3. This year, Senator Burns will run for reelection.

4. Barbara said, "Let me know when you are off the phone."

5. Beth's new car is a black Dodge Daytona, which she purchased at the Dodge dealer in New York City.

6. Mike and Jackie are both graduates of Edison High School.

7. Glaciers from the Ice Age still exist.

Exercise – Writing Skills

1. **(C)** Evidence for Lincoln's feelings suggests that he was "saddened" by the bitter fighting, and that he had "worked hard to prevent a split." In addition, he felt that these soldiers had not died "in vain," or uselessly. Consequently, only (C) could be correct.

2. **(B)** The adjectival form "second," not the adverbial form "secondly," is appropriate here, since it modifies a noun and not a verb.

3. **(B)** The opening verbal phrase is a dangling modifier. "Prevention" is not "faced" with anything; Lincoln is. All the other choices are standard English sentences.

4. **(C)** "With the outbreak . . ." is a prepositional phrase that is stopped with a period [.]. It has no subject or verb and is not a standard English sentence. All the rest are correct English.

5. **(C)** Since the pattern of the paragraph is to show evidence for how Dr. Goddard developed his rocket technology over time, only (C) could be correct. Transitions that show logical connections ("consequently," "thus,") are not appropriate. Also, choices (A), (B), and (D) are all abstract statements, not evidence for Goddard's developmental progress. Only (C) meets both these requirements of the chronological pattern using concrete evidence to show Goddard's progress.

6. **(A)** The phrase "at one time . . ." is a nonrestrictive unit that is not necessary to the basic meaning of the sentence; consequently, both commas are needed. The commas for (B) and (D) are necessary to set off introductory or qualifying phrases. No commas are needed in (B) since the phrase that follows is a direct adjectival qualification of what kind of rockets they are (as we know them today). Thus, no comma of separation is needed.

7. **(B)** This is just a long phrase; it has no subject or verb. (C) is an atypical, but rhetorically correct and standard, English sentence. Many sentences in English begin with "And." The other choices are standard subject/verb independent sentence units.

8. **(A)** This word is too general for such a specific informational context. (B) should remain because it is the exact, or first, phrase the writer discusses. (C) need not be changed because only a synonym such as "real" would be needed, but the meaning would remain the same. (D) is all right because the writer points not to any specific study, research, or development done, but to all that type of "work" in general.

9. **(B)** The writer uses evidence in the form of illustrative examples to demonstrate that the executive woman in business is everywhere. (A) is incorrect for this reason. (C) is incorrect because the writer clearly states that she is no longer the "pariah," or outcast, of the business world. (D) is clearly incorrect because it stands in direct contradiction to what the writer's examples demonstrate of the ubiquity of her presence and the value of her paycheck.

10. (C)   It is not the work force that is "for the better," but the situation for men. This is also supported by the rest of the evidence offered in the paragraph. The other sentences have their modifying phrases directly related to the idea they qualify.

11. (B)   The writer is comparing before and after the appearance of women in management; only two things — therefore, the comparative form, not the superlative, is correct: "greater." (A), (C), and (D) are all incorrect responses; they have no comparative adjectives, just adverbs used as qualifiers, e.g., "overly." These are used in a standard way.

12. (B)   It is a run-on sentence, incorrectly punctuated with a comma after "families" instead of a period or a semicolon. The rest of the choices are all standard sentences.

13. (C)   (A) is not correct because, although the writer states that watching television doesn't demand much imagination, s/he never says that the entertainment itself is unimaginative. (B) is not correct because it is not the best representation of the writer's point of view, but only part of it. (D) is incorrect because the third paragraph clearly supports the notion that television is neither demanding nor very educational.

14. (D)   Has an incorrect agreement between "kids" and "does." Kids (they) do (something). All the other sentences use standard English syntax.

15. (D)   The sentence is a rhetorical clause that begins with a subordinating conjunction, "because." Consequently, it cannot stand alone as a complete standard sentence. The rest are standard.

16. (B)   Unless the writer specifies with the correct noun who exactly is drinking the orange juice, it could be either the mother or the baby: both are female. The rest are standard as is.

NEW JERSEY
HSPA
High School Proficiency Assessment in
Language Arts

Practice
Test 1

HSPA
Language Arts

Practice Test 1
(See page 179 for answer sheets.)

TIME: Total Testing Time – Approximately 3 hours
Approximate section timing is as follows:
30 minutes for Writing: Speculate (picture prompt)
50 minutes for Reading: Narrative
60 minutes for Writing: Persuade
45 minutes for Reading: Persuasive
25 minutes for Writing: Revise/Edit

Note: The test is given over a two- or three-day period. Testing times and section lengths are approximate, and will vary from administration to administration.

Writing: speculate (picture prompt) – 30 mins.

Reprinted, by permission, from Ravi Kalia, *Chandigarh: In Search of an Identity*, page 97.
© 1987 by the Board of Trustees, Southern Illinois University.

Writing Task:

Look carefully at the photograph on the previous page. How would you characterize this scene? What does looking at this photo make you think or feel? Write an essay in which you imagine what kind of "story" might accompany this picture.

Reading (narrative) – 50 mins.

Introduction: In the following selection from an 1861 story by Rebecca Harding Davis, the first-person narrator directly addresses and questions the reader, presenting a startling view of life in the iron mills. Feel free to make marginal notes and/or underline as you read the text and answer the test questions.

LIFE IN THE IRON MILLS

A cloudy day: do you know what that is in a town of iron-works? The sky sank down before dawn, muddy, flat, immovable. The air is thick, clammy with the breath of crowded human beings. It stifles me. I open the window, and, looking out, can scarcely see through the rain the grocer's shop opposite, where a crowd of drunken Irishmen are puffing Lynchburg tobacco in their pipes. I can detect the scent through all the foul smells ranging loose in the air.

The idiosyncrasy of this town is smoke. It rolls sullenly in slow folds from the great chimneys of the iron-foundries, and settles down in black, slimy pools on the muddy streets. Smoke on the wharfs, smoke on the dingy boats, on the yellow river,—clinging in a coating of greasy soot to the house-front, the two faded poplars, the faces of the passersby. The long train of mules, dragging masses of pig-iron through the narrow street, have a foul vapor hanging to their reeking sides. Here, inside, is a little broken figure of an angel pointing upward from the mantel-shelf; but even its wings are covered with smoke, clotted and black. Smoke everywhere! A dirty canary chirps desolately in a cage beside me. Its dream of green fields and sunshine is a very old dream,—almost worn out, I think.

From the back-window I can see a narrow brick-yard sloping down to the river-side, strewed with rain-butts and tubs. The river, dull and tawny-colored, (*la belle rivière*!) drags itself sluggishly along, tired of the heavy weight of boats and coal-barges. What wonder? When I was a child, I used to fancy a look of weary, dumb appeal upon the face of the negro-like river slavishly bearing its burden day after day. Something of the same idle notion comes to me to-day, when from the street-window I look on the slow stream of human life creeping past, night and morning, to the great mills. Masses of men, with dull, besotted faces bent to the ground, sharpened here and there by pain or cunning; skin and muscle and flesh begrimed with smoke and ashes; stooping all night over boiling caldrons of metal, laired by day in dens of drunkenness and infamy; breathing from infancy to death an air saturated with fog and grease and soot, vileness for soul and body. What do you make of a case like that, amateur psychologist? You call it an altogether serious thing to be alive: to these men it is a drunken jest, a joke,—horrible to angels perhaps, to them commonplace enough. My fancy about the river was an idle one: it is no type of such a life. What if it be stagnant and slimy here? It knows that beyond there waits for it odorous sunlight,—quaint old gardens, dusky with soft, green foliage of apple-trees, and flushing crimson with roses,—air, and fields, and mountains. The future of the Welsh puddler passing just now is not so pleasant. To be stowed away, after his grimy work is done, in a hole in the muddy graveyard, and after that,—*not* air, nor green fields, nor curious roses.

Can you see how foggy the day is? As I stand here, idly tapping the window-pane, and looking out through the rain at the dirty back-yard and the coalboats below, fragments of an old story float up before me,—a story of this old house into which I happened to come to-day. You may think it is a tiresome story enough, as foggy as the day, sharpened by no sudden flashes of pain or pleasure.—I know: only the outline of a dull life, that long since, with thousands of dull lives like its own, was vainly lived and lost: thousands of them,—massed, vile, slimy lives, like those of the torpid lizards in yonder stagnant water-butt.—Lost? There is a curious point for you to settle, my friend, who study psychology in a lazy, *dilettante* way. Stop a moment. I am going to be honest. This is what I want you to do. I want you to hide your disgust, take no heed to your clean clothes, and come right down with me,—here, into the thickest of the fog and mud and foul effluvia. I want you to hear this story. There is a secret down here, in this nightmare fog, that has lain dumb for centuries: I want to make it a real thing to you. You, Egoist, Pantheist, or Arminian, busy in making straight paths for your feet on the hills, do not see it clearly,—this terrible question which men here have gone mad and died trying to answer. I dare not put this secret into words. I told you it was dumb. These men, going by with drunken faces and brains full of unawakened power, do not ask it of Society or of God. Their lives ask it; their deaths ask it. There is no reply. I will tell you plainly that I have a great hope; and I bring it to you to be tested. It is this: that this terrible dumb question is its own reply; that it is not the sentence of death we think it, but, from the very extremity of its darkness, the most solemn prophecy which the world has known of the Hope to come. I dare make my meaning no clearer, but will only tell my story. It will, perhaps, seem to you as foul and dark as this thick vapor about us, and as pregnant with death; but if your eyes are free as mine are to look deeper, no perfume-tinted dawn will be so fair with promise of the day that shall surely come.

1. The opening sentence of the passage does all of the following EXCEPT

    (A) draw the listener into the passage.

    (B) imply that the listener belongs to a different world than that being described here.

    (C) challenge the listener's knowledge and experience.

    (D) reveal to the listener the speaker's lack of knowledge about her subject matter.

2. It can be inferred that "Lynchburg tobacco," referred to early in the piece, is

    (A) the preferred brand of Irishmen.

    (B) detrimental to its smokers' health.

    (C) a particularly inferior brand.

    (D) obtainable at the "grocer's shop."

3. The expository, or explanatory, technique of the third paragraph is best described as

    (A) question and answer.

    (B) chronological order.

    (C) cause and effect.

    (D) comparison/contrast.

4. Which word BEST describes the speaker's tone?

    (A) Philosophical   (C) Comforting

    (B) Despairing   (D) Detached

5. Considering the passage as a whole, the "terrible question which men here have gone mad and died trying to answer" can best be identified as:

    (A) How can the life of the ironworks town laborer be bettered?

    (B) What is the meaning of life?

    (C) How can the pollution from the ironworks be lessened?

    (D) What is the responsibility of the upper to the lower classes?

6. Which of the following does the speaker NOT allude to as a characteristic of the ironworkers' lives?

    (A) Breathing polluted air

    (B) Smoke- and ash-covered skin

    (C) Peaceful sleep

    (D) Unused potential

7. Based on the conclusion of this passage, it can be inferred that the speaker believes that

    (A) human existence is pointless.

    (B) social reform is near.

    (C) afterlife is the ultimate hope.

    (D) men live more desperate lives than women.

8. The story that the speaker will tell in the rest of the narrative is most probably

    (A) a bitter life lived without redress.

    (B) an example of a terrible life ending with an anticipated unearthly reward.

    (C) a retelling of his/her life in the ironworks town.

    (D) a futuristic tale of life to come in the ironworks town.

9. The author describes the town near the iron mills as

    (A) a town of strict behavior codes and with smoking, drinking, and uncleanness almost non-existent.

(B) a town with a very sparse population.

(C) a town with happy workers eager to complete their work day and to enjoy the pleasures of the nearby river.

(D) a town on the brink of change.

10. The first paragraph is in

(A) the third person.

(B) the second person.

(C) the first person.

(D) a combination of the first and second person.

11. Discuss TWO reasons why the narrator might directly address and question the reader.

- Do you think that the narrator's strategy of address is effective?

- Cite specific details from the story to support and explain your views.

12. Describe two details that the author uses to help the reader maintain hope for the town near the iron mills.

- Cite each example.

- Explain why each is effective.

Writing: persuade – 60 mins.

Many scholars note the decline of interest in literature written before the twentieth century. A diminishing number of students pursue studies in classical, medieval, and even Renaissance literature. In an essay written to an English teacher, argue whether you feel that the trend of studying modern versus past literature is commendable or contemptible. Reflect on modern culture and the effects of literature upon it. Discuss the advantages/disadvantages of a study that excludes or minimizes the literature of earlier periods. Finally, draw upon your own exposure to and attitude toward modern and past literatures, respectively.

Reading: persuasive – 45 mins.

Introduction: The passages you are about to read are remarks made by a U.S. senator on the floor of the U.S. Senate during consideration of Senate Joint Resolution 73 in March of 1984. Senators, like other speakers, present arguments orally in order to persuade listeners to understand a certain point of view and to support their position when voting.

The passage presents the remarks made by Senator Mark O. Hatfield, Republican of Oregon, on March 8, 1984.

You may write notes or underline information as you read and answer the questions that follow.

Should the U.S. Constitution be Amended to Permit School Prayer?—Con

The central question in this debate as I see it is simply:

How can we adequately protect the right of our people to be free from having an alien religious practice forced upon their children by governmental action, but at the same time allow them to freely exercise their own religion without government hostility. In my view, Senate Joint resolution 73 fails to measure up to this crucial standard.

Objections to the pending prayer amendment that I wish to comment on:

First, I think if you look at the pending prayer amendment you will find that amendment looks to the state, to the teacher, and to the school board to initiate, orchestrate, structure, and organize prayer or religious activity in our public schools.

Second, the pending prayer amendment fundamentally alters the careful balance in the first amendment between the free exercise clause and the prohibition against the establishment of religion. When our Constitution was established, no other nation provided so carefully to prevent the combination of the power of religion with the power of the national government.

Third, the pending prayer amendment violates another central premise of the first amendment, and that is that government should be prohibited from favoring certain religions at the expense of others.

What is really behind the school prayer controversy, we might legitimately ask.

Since that decision [that removed prayer from the classroom], the Supreme Court's ruling has been claimed for the deteriorating quality of public education, for the breakdown of the American family, for the decay in moral principles, and abdication of governmental institutions to the norm of secular humanism.

There is an alternative. The first amendment to the U.S. Constitution sets limits on the ability of government to promote, establish, and inculcate religious beliefs in public schools students—but it sets no limit on student-initiated prayer or religious discussion during noninstructional time periods. Instead of concentrating upon a school prayer amendment, I urge my colleagues to devote their energies to rooting out ridiculous barriers that have been erected to forbid voluntary meetings of students who seek to meet and pray in nondisruptive ways.

A growing number of federal courts have expanded the prohibitions on the sponsorship by the state of religious activity in public schools to encompass equal access policies adopted by school boards as well as student requests to meet on their own time before or after school hours for prayer, devotional reading or religious discussions. These prohibitions are hostile to the rights of religious expression and, in my view, violate the free speech rights of students.

In the Lubbock School Board case, 23 senators joined with me in filing a friend of the court brief asking the Supreme Court to grant a hearing and reverse the decision. In that brief, we argued that:

"Neither legislation nor a constitutional amendment is required to permit a school to open its facilities for all appropriate student-initiated and student-managed activities including, if the students wish, religious activities. The Constitution already so provides. The Establishment, Free Exercise and Free Speech clauses of the First Amendment require treatment of such activities in a neutral manner. Consequently, public schools properly may allow students equal access to school facilities for voluntary, extra-curricular, religious speech and assembly."

As the original sponsor of equal access legislation that was introduced on September 17, 1982, I want the Senate to know that I am adamantly opposed to the idea of including equal access language in a constitutional amendment for it undercuts the very heart of my legislation. A student's right to gather together with others for prayer and religious discussion is inherent in the first amendment right now. It comes under the protections of free speech and the freedom of association when an open forum is established by the school. Including this language in a constitutional amendment will significantly reverse the program that has been made in pending litigation and puts a stamp of approval behind the logic of Brandon and Lubbock opinions. Instead of ill-conceived constitutional amendments, let us proceed to a simple statute that provides a judicial remedy to aggrieved high school students.

Some 26 senators have joined me in offering Senate bill 815 which would make clear that secondary school students have the right to meet voluntarily during noninstructional time periods for prayer or devotional reading. S. 815 has united a number of senators who differ on constitutional amendments that permit school sponsored prayer or statutory approaches which deny jurisdiction to federal courts to decide school prayer cases. But the sponsors of S. 815 agree that the constitution does not allow our public schools to be hostile to religion.

S. 815 also has the support of religious groups that have opposed school prayer amendments. S. 815 can pass this Congress and provide a reasonable solution to the school prayer controversy.

The focus of S. 815 is on student-initiated religious activities instead of the government inculcation of religious belief. Given the strong bipartisan support that this bill has received in the Senate, I urge the Senate to approve S. 815.

We have had a case that went to the Supreme Court in which students who had asked to use public university facilities for religious purposes had been denied the right to use such facilities. That case was taken to the U.S. Supreme Court, and the U.S. Supreme Court ruled in the Widmar case that once a public university or a college had established the right of students to voluntarily organize and use public facilities for student associations of camera clubs, drama clubs, music clubs, or whatever else, that the same university that established the right of forum could not dictate the content of the forum and, therefore, students would be denied their constitutional right to use those same facilities for religious purposes that they could use for every other purpose. Now the Court has ruled on that.

What I attempted to do in S. 815 was merely to apply that same constitutional right that has been extended to university students in public institutions to students at the secondary level.

So those who think they are promoting religious activity, those who think they are promoting the possibility of spiritual renewal by some kind of civil religion in our public schools, ought to realize that they are also raising some serious questions and confusion among those activities that are now in place and functioning without question in our public universities.

So I oppose the constitutional amendments—all of them—that relate to school prayer, whether it is silent meditation or anything else. It is all part of our civil religion, not spiritual, Biblical faith.

1. Which of the following objections does Senator Hatfield NOT make regarding the proposed school prayer amendment?

    (A) It alters the First Amendment balance between free exercise and protection from religious establishment.

(B) It violates the First Amendment prohibition against favoring one religion over others.

(C) It looks to the state to organize religious activity in schools.

(D) It would require students to say prayers that they might not agree with.

2. What does Senator Hatfield propose instead of a constitutional amendment in order to address prayer in public schools?

(A) He does not propose an alternative.

(B) He proposes a Supreme Court case to redress the violation of secondary school students' free speech rights.

(C) He proposes Senate bill 815, which would uphold the right of secondary school students to have voluntary prayer activities during non-instructional time.

(D) He suggests adding Senate bill 815 onto the constitutional amendment on school prayer.

3. Senator Hatfield draws upon several kinds of evidence to support his argument. What kind of evidence does he NOT use in his remarks?

(A) Letters from public school students

(B) Quotations from legal sources

(C) His own view of the issues

(D) Reference to previous Supreme Court decisions

4. Based on his remarks regarding school prayer, which would Senator Hatfield support?

(A) A state-sponsored hour of prayer in public schools

(B) A prayer club at a public high school

(C) A district rule forbidding religious gatherings on school property

(D) Religious readings during instructional time in a public high school

5. What resource would be the best place to look for the *most current perspectives on* school prayer?

    (A) A weekly news magazine

    (B) A religion textbook

    (C) An encyclopedia

    (D) Congressional records from the 1990s

6. Senator Hatfield

    (A) voices three chief objections to Senate bill 815.

    (B) advocates the idea of including equal access language in a constitutional amendment.

    (C) notes that students have the right to gather together with others for prayer—a right inherent in the First Amendment.

    (D) distinguishes between the right of secondary school students to meet voluntarily during non-instructional time for prayer and that of elementary school students to do the same.

7. The word "abdication" as it is used in paragraph 8 means

    (A) abandonment.

    (B) hostility.

    (C) taking away or kidnapping.

    (D) sensitivity.

8. As shown in the second-to-last paragraph, what are Senator Hatfield's feelings regarding "those who think they are promoting religious activity, those who think they are promoting the possibility of spiritual renewal"?

    (A) He thinks they are admirable.

    (B) He thinks they are well-intentioned but misguided.

    (C) He thinks they are ineffective but harmless.

    (D) He thinks they have concealed, harmful objectives.

9. Senator Hatfield mentions that the Supreme Court affirmed the right of public university students to use school facilities for religious purposes. What is his opinion on this right?

   (A) He thinks it is unnecessary.

   (B) He thinks it will lead to future problems.

   (C) He thinks the right should be extended to secondary school students.

   (D) He thinks it is unconsitutional.

10. Which of the following BEST expresses the central idea of this passage?

   (A) The school prayer amendment is flawed, and the Senate should instead approve a bill that affirms the right of students to meet for prayer during nonistructional periods.

   (B) The school prayer amendment must be passed, along with a bill that affirms the rights of students to meet for prayer during noninstructional periods.

   (C) The Supreme Court has clearly decided that prayer on school grounds is unconstitutional under any circumstances.

   (D) Federal courts have expanded the prohibitions against state-sponsored religion.

   DIRECTIONS: For questions 11 and 12, write your answer in the space provided in the back of the book. Refer to the persuasive text by Senator Hatfield. Address all parts of the question.

11. Describe TWO strategies used by the senator to persuade his audience to agree with him.

   • Think about the senator's remarks and explain why each strategy is effective.

12. Assume that a group of students want to pray in a high school. How should this be possible from Senator Hatfield's point of view? What might be the limits he would want on this activity? Explain why you answered as you did.

Writing: revise/edit – 25 mins.

Andre's class was asked to write about their views on the environment in their daily journals. He has asked you to edit and revise his essay. Feel free to make marks in the text as you read, revise, and edit. Alternatively, you may rewrite the essay to include your corrections.

The environment is something that I worrying about. It hits me the most when instead of trees or plants in fields I see huge industrial plants instead. It amazes me how much smoke come out of these huge monsters.

Not that I'm the best environmentalist. While I do recycle glass and alumnium cans, and I make sure to turn off lights, and appliances, there are times that I'm too lazy to be active in saving the earth. I think of all the people like me who don't care if they throw garbage anywhere or if they waste water. I try to imagine how it all adds up. The picture is overwelming.

Yet that doesn't seem like it would even compare to things like cutting down the rain forests or destroying the ozone layer. There are so many species of animal life that we will never even see because of these devastations. More worse things seem to happen every day. Yet these things seem so so far away from me that it's very hard to imagine.

I guess that someday these personal and industrial offenses to our world will add up against us, We seem to be ruining our world. What would it be like without clean air and grass? I imagine it would be like acid rain falling on a lot of metal.

HSPA
PRACTICE TEST 1

ANSWER KEY

Reading: narrative

1.	(D)	6.	(C)	11.	Essay
2.	(C)	7.	(C)	12.	Essay
3.	(D)	8.	(B)		
4.	(A)	9.	(D)		
5.	(B)	10.	(D)		

Reading: persuasive

1.	(D)	6.	(C)	11.	Essay
2.	(C)	7.	(A)	12.	Essay
3.	(A)	8.	(B)		
4.	(B)	9.	(C)		
5.	(A)	10.	(A)		

DETAILED EXPLANATIONS
OF ANSWERS

HSPA LANGUAGE ARTS

TEST 1

Writing: speculate (picture prompt)

GOOD RESPONSE

Sanjay was excited. The new governmental offices, just completed, were the site of a meeting that was for only a very small number of selected families. Sanjay's family was one, and he was so proud that he ran and twirled around the enormous wide open spaces in front of the government office building. He was too young to be admitted into the meeting with his mother and the District Appropriator of Human Resources, but he was sure that it had gone well and that his family had been commended for their responsible conduct.

As his mother led him away from the gigantic buildings and back towards their home, he asked if he would be told what happened in the meeting. Though everyone remarked that he was remarkably bright for his age, his mother told him that he would not understand, and that it was a matter for adults. But he asked and asked and begged and begged, until finally she told him that she and his father would tell him that evening.

That evening after dinner, his father and mother came to Sanjay's side. Their faces were serious and cautious. His father put on his glasses and began to speak.

"Sanjay," he said, "this is a big surprise for us. But the government has informed us that they need our services, and we are proud to do our duty. This family is to be relocated to the new colony at the bottom of the sea." Sanjay was overcome with shock and surprise, and he became so excited that he fainted. When he came to, his father was standing over him grinning sheepishly.

"I'm sorry, son. I didn't think you would faint away like that. We are not really going under the sea."

"What?" Sanjay said. He was very confused.

"The official just wanted to talk to us about a tax refund. But you bothered your mother so much about it, I wanted to tell you something very shocking so that you would find out that there are some things you don't want to know about."

Sanjay was relieved to know that he would not have to move under the ocean. However, he now realized that there were many things he did not quite understand about his parents, and he was content to let it stay that way.

Features of the Good Response

This response is free of mechanical errors. The author suggests an interesting possible idea for what is happening. It is a creative expansion of the picture, in which the author is both attentive to details and willing to offer some novel ways for thinking about its content. The organization is clear, and the narrative progresses logically. There is an overall sense of focus, and the sentences are structured properly.

POOR RESPONSE

This photo is black and white. It is a picture with people in it. There are seven main people. In the center. There are other people to the sides, and its hard too count 'em all. There is a building on the left that has pillars and balconies. Maybe it's apartments. I can't tell. It doesn't look like anyone is really doing anything interesting. The buildings to the right are harder to see. I don't know what they are but they aren't very nice. Some are children, some are adults maybe they all live in the apartments, if they are apartments. It looks like you could play football in the middle of the street they are on.

The building to the left is maybe a mall or something because there might be some signs or something. I can't really see, though. Maybe it's a deli. Malls aren't usually built that way, so this would be a very unusual mall. The people in the center are holding hands so they might be a family.

Features of the Poor Response

This is a poorly written essay. There are several mechanical errors, such as the use of "too" instead of "to," and "its" instead of "it's" in the fifth sentence. The use of "em" is not appropriate for a formal writing assignment. There are also several sentence construction errors, including a run-on and a fragment in the first paragraph. The essay is very poorly organized. Thoughts are randomly inserted throughout. For instance, the author is describing the people in the first paragraph, then talks about the building. There is an abrupt change back to describing the people at the end. The author is also overly concerned with simply pointing out "facts" from the photo—i.e., the number of people in the center—and not sufficiently concerned with the kind of creative expansion called for in the directions.

Reading: narrative

1.   **(D)**   The speaker brings the listener into the passage (A) by directly asking him/her "do you know . . . " and (B) by immediately providing the answer makes it clear that the listener could not possibly have firsthand knowledge (C) of life in an ironworks. (D) is correct because it misinterprets the intent of the question; the speaker's swift and detailed response indicates that information is not actually sought from the audience.

2.   **(C)**   The speaker implies that Lynchburg tobacco is inferior (C) by having it smoked by men who are loitering, drunken, and, judging by these states, presumably poor. The smoking of this tobacco by this group does not imply that all Irishmen smoke it or even that these particular men prefer it to other brands (A). There is no suggestion of tobacco's effect upon its smokers (B). One cannot assume that the smokers bought their tobacco at the grocer's shop simply because they are loitering outside it (D).

3.   **(D)**   This paragraph compares and contrasts (D) the river and the ironworks laborer, both "working" slavishly, but one bearing hope of a better future. The paragraph does not present a series of questions and answers (A). The narration is not chronological (B) because the speaker moves from present to past to present to future. There is no cause and effect (C).

4.   **(A)**   Of the answers given, philosophical best describes the speaker's reflective, questioning tone. The speaker is neither totally (B) despairing nor wholly (C) comforting as she presents the town of ironworks. (D) is also incorrect, since the speaker is not detached from her subject matter, but very much engaged.

5.   **(B)**   The very lives and deaths of the workers (paragraph 3) are lives so terrible and hopeless and deaths so unremarkable that they ask, "What is the point of existence?" (B). In order for (A) to be correct, there would have to be suggestions for concrete reform, rather than abstract

promises "of the day that shall surely come." Pollution (C) is indeed a problem, but it is a backdrop to the problems of the workers. While it is implied that the reader is of higher socioeconomic status than the worker, there is no blame given or responsibility attributed for the condition of the workers (D).

6. **(C)** The speaker does not mention the ironworkers' sleep and, given the other aspects of their lives, the reader can imagine that their sleep is not peaceful. Paragraph three discusses how the men (A) breathe "air saturated with fog and grease and soot" and describes their (B) "skin . . . begrimed with smoke and ashes." (D) is also incorrect, since the speaker does allude to the men's unused potential in paragraph four when she mentions their "brains full of unawakened power."

7. **(C)** The speaker states that the question answers itself and is "the most solemn prophecy . . . of the Hope to come" (paragraph 4); in addition, the story to be told "will be so fair with promise of the day that shall surely come." These phrases indicate that there is a reason for human life [ruling out (A)], and their religious connotations imply that this reason is a "life" after human toil (C). The predicted relief is described in vague and religious terms, not in socioeconomic language (B). Although only the terrible lives of men are described, the omission of women does not imply that they fare better (D).

8. **(B)** The speaker describes the projected story as "the outline of a dull life, that long since . . . vainly lived and lost" (paragraph 4); its conclusion in the past rules out (C) and (D). (A) is incorrect because a hard life without remedy holds none of the hope the speaker foretells. The speaker implies that the story will be dark but will end with promise of otherworldly redress (B).

9. **(D)** is the best answer. The writer suggests that there is hope ahead for the residents of the town near the iron mills. For the better time to come, there must be some changes in the iron mills. (D) suggests that the change is inherent for the town. (A) is not the right answer; there seems to be no strict behavior codes in the dirty city with its dirty, drunken citizens who are adding more smoke to the already polluted air. The town is crowded; (B) would not be an acceptable answer. The passage describes the drudgery of the workers; the river is not an appealing place. (C) is not the best choice.

10. **(D)** is the correct answer. The use of the words *you* and *I* indicate both first person and second person. The use of *he, she,* and *it* indicates third person; these pronouns are not used; answer (A) is not appropriate. (B) is a correct answer; (C) is a correct answer. Because both are correct, only (D) allows the reader to choose both of these answers.

11. As you study the two sample responses below, notice that the good response (representing a score of 3 or 4) discusses TWO separate reasons with support from the story and explanation of the narrator's effectiveness. The poor response (representing a score of 1 or 2) presents ONE literal reason with weak explanation.

GOOD RESPONSE

The author of the story has the first person narrator address the reader in order to get the reader's attention. The narrator's story about the lives of ironworkers is serious and demands serious consideration. Thus, the reader pays attention when he or she is told: "Stop a moment. I am going to be honest. This is what I want you to do." The reader, once addressed in this way, becomes more active and is drawn into the narrative. The narrator's direct address not only gets the reader's attention but also conveys the narrator's own passion and urgency about her subject matter. She confesses, for example, "I have a great hope; and I bring it to you to be tested." The narrator has a clear purpose and the direct address conveys that purpose effectively. I think that by speaking to the reader, the narrator makes sure that her words connect with the reader and cause the reader to think and act in a new way.

POOR RESPONSE

The narrator talks to the reader directly so that the reader will follow her: "come right down with me." The reader is invited into the story, but has to hide disgust and be ready for dirt. In this way, the narrator's strategy is effective. The reader follows the events more easily.

12. As you study the two sample responses below, notice that the good response (representing a score of 3 or 4) has an opening and closing. It is well-developed and has a logical progression of ideas. There are no errors in usage, sentence construction, or mechanics. The paragraphs answer the question's requirements: to cite examples and explain why each is effective. The poor response (representing a score of 1 or 2) is uncertain in addressing the topic; there is as much emphasis on the pessimism as there is on the optimism. Furthermore, the poor response contains many errors in spelling and usage.

GOOD RESPONSE

The author of "Life in the Iron Mills" ends with a message of hope for the reader. To create this optimistic ending, the writer uses several devices. In my opinion, two are particularly effective in generating an expectation for a better day for the town and the people near the iron works.

One thing that the writer does is to encourage the reader to look deeper than the physical features of the town. The writer notes that there is promise of a "day that shall surely come." This is an effective technique because the writer admits having first-hand knowledge of the town; if the writer is convinced that the future is positive, the reader feels comfortable in feeling that way also.

A second effective device that the writer uses is to tell the reader plainly that she has a great hope. She further emphasizes this hope by noting that the lives of the workers ask for power. This plea from those who have given their best to the iron mills helps to convince the reader that the price for a better life has been paid. This device of noting that their lives and deaths ask for a better life justifies hope. With this price having been paid, the town is due a better life; this is a good way to persuade the reader of the legitimacy of this hope.

Particularly because of two examples of hope, because of the convincing way that the writer uses them, and because of the price that has already been paid, the reader is left with a feeling of optimism.

POOR RESPONSE

The writer did not convince the reader that better times are ahead. The passage was depressing. One feels sad after reading it. I felt almost as sad as I did after reading about city life that Charles Dickens depicts.

Speaking of foggy days, stagnant water, drunkenness grease and soot. These were depressing. There is nothing to convince the reader that it is not a "sentence of death."

The mention of crimsen roses and green apple trees brings hope of deth. Good times not ahead. Because of two examples of hope, because of the convincing way that the writer uses them, and because of the price that has already been paid, the reader is left with a feeling of optimism/pessimism.

Writing: persuade

GOOD RESPONSE

The Literature of the Past

The direction of modern literary scholarship points toward an alarming conclusion. The depreciation of the literary study of bygone periods is a sign of two disturbing trends. First, scholars are avoiding more difficult study in preference to what seems light or facile. Furthermore, the neglect of the literature of former eras is a denial of the contribution that past authors have made toward modern literature. This is not to suggest that all scholars who study modern literature do so because they are either intimidated by past literature or do not appreciate its value. However, the shrinking minority of past literary scholarship is a clear indication that intimidation and awe of past conventions are deterrents to many students of literature.

The dread associated with past literature reflects poorly upon our society. The attempts to simplify literature to accommodate simpler audiences has resulted in a form of literary deflation. The less society taxes its audience's minds, the less comprehensive those unexercised minds become. Information and ideas are now transmitted to the average man through the shallow medium of television programming. Modern students are evolving from this medium, and the gap separating them from the complexity of the classics is continuing to grow.

Once more, it is important to stress that this essay does not seek to diminish students of modern literature. The only demand this argument makes upon modern students is that they supplement their study with significant portions of the classics from which all subsequent literature has been derived, whether consciously or unconsciously. Failure to do so is an act akin to denying the importance of history itself. Like history, literature exists as an evolutionary process; modern literature can only have come into existence through the development of past literature.

Concerning the relative complexity of the classics to modern literature, the gap is not so great as one may think. Surely, one who glances at the works of Shakespeare or Milton without prior exposure will be daunted by them. However, a disciplined mind can overcome the comprehensive barriers erected over the past few centuries through persistence and perseverance.

Unfortunately, the ability to overcome the barriers to past literature may eventually become obsolete. The more frequently students select their courses of study through fear rather than interest, the wider the literary gap will become, until the pampered minds of all future readers will prove unequal to the task of reading the literature of our fathers. The more frequently students deny the usefulness of the literature antedating this century, the more frequently they deny their own literary heritage, the more probable it will become for modern literature's structure to crumble through lack of firm foundation.

Features of the Good Response

The paper's topic and the writer's viewpoint are both well laid out in the first paragraph. The two trends described by the author in the topic paragraph are explored in deeper detail throughout the essay. The language and style fit the writer's audience. The style is formal, but possesses a personalized voice.

The essay follows the course presented in the topic paragraph, reemphasizing major points such as the writer's reluctance to condemn all modern scholars. This emphasis is not straight repetition, but carries different viewpoints and evidence for the writer's argument. The digression on television in the second paragraph neatly rounds off the writer's overall concern for cultural consequences of past literature's depreciation.

The writer follows the suggestions of the writing assignment closely, structuring his essay around the reflections and discussions listed therein. Each paragraph bears an example to lend authority to the writer's argument. The second paragraph uses the theory of television's vegetative influence. The third paragraph utilizes the evolutionary equality of history. The fourth paragraph evokes names that the reader can relate to in terms of comprehensive difficulty.

Many transitional conventions are utilized: "Once more . . ."; "Concerning the relative complexity . . ."; "Unfortunately . . ." The examples throughout the paragraphs have a pointed direction. The conclusion paragraph rounds off the argument with a premonition of future calamity should its warning go unheeded.

The sentences are standardized and vary in form, although some passive constructions ("will be daunted," "the more probable it will become") may have been avoided. The repetition of "the more frequently" in the final paragraph is particularly effective and pointed.

Words are chosen to offer variety. "Past literature" is supplemented by "literary study of bygone days" and "the literature of former eras." Phrasing is consistent and standard, although the third sentence of the second paragraph ("The less society taxes...the less comprehensive...") is slightly awkward, though the repetition does achieve some effect.

POOR RESPONSE

Modern literature is no better than past literature, and vice-versa. It is interest that matters. If people aren't interested in the past, then so be it. A famous man once said "To each his own". I agree.

For example, you can see that books are getting easier and easier to understand. This is a good thing, because more knowledge may be comunicated this way. Comunication is what literature is all about: Some people comunicate with the past, and others with the present.

I communicate with the present. I'm not saying we all should. It's all up to your point of view. When a scholer chooses past over present, or vice-versa, that's his perogative. It doesn't make him better or worse than anybody else. We should all learn to accept each other's point of view.

When I read someone like Fitzgerald or Tolkien, I get a different feeling than Shakespeare. Shakespeare can inspire many people, but I just don't get that certain feeling from his plays. "The Hobbit," "The Great Gatsby," "Catcher in the Rye," and "Of Mice and Men." These are all great classics from this century. We should be proud of them. However, some people prefer "The Trojan War" and "Beowulf." Let them have it. Remember: "To each his own."

Features of the Poor Response

The writer misconstrues the topic and writes about the relative worth of modern and past literature. The topic does not call for a judgment of period literatures; it calls for a study on the way in which they are studied. His personal style is too familiarized; it is unclear to whom the essay is addressed.

The writer seems to contradict his own points at times, favoring modern literature rather than treating the subject as objective as he had proposed. It is clear that the writer's train of thought shifted during the essay. This was covered up by ending with the catch phrase, "to each his own."

The writer attempts to angle his argument in different ways by presenting such concepts as "communication" and "point of view." However, his thought processes are abrupt and underdeveloped.

There is neither direction nor logical flow in the essay. One point follows the next without any transition or connection. All three persons are used to prove his argument: the writer resorts to "I," "you," and "a famous man." It is clear there is no overall thesis guiding the essay.

Some sentences follow standard formation. Sentence three of the final paragraph is a fragment. The sentences are short and choppy, as is the thought they convey. Too many sentences are merely brief remarks on the preceding statements (e.g., "I agree"; "Let them have it"; etc.). These are not appropriate because they do not evoke new thought. The reference to Shakespeare in the first sentence of the final paragraph implies more than the writer intended. It should read: "than when I read Shakespeare."

Many words are repeated without any attempt to supply synonyms (e.g., "communication," "past"). Colloquial expressions are widespread and should be avoided. *The Trojan War* is evidently an improper reference to Homer's *Iliad*.

Reading: persuasive

1. **(D)** The school prayer amendment only proposes voluntary prayer; there is no suggestion of forcing students to pray. Thus, Senator Hatfield cannot object on the grounds that students will be forced to say prayers they do not agree with. Senator Hatfield does object to (A) altering the First Amendment balance between free exercise and protection from religious establishment, (B) violating the First Amendment prohibition against favoring one religion over another, and (C) looking to the state to organize religious activity in school. Since the question asked which objection the senator did NOT make, (A), (B), and (C) are incorrect.

2. **(C)** Hatfield, along with other senators, proposes Senate bill 815. (A) is incorrect; Hatfield does indeed propose an alternative to a constitutional amendment. (B) is incorrect; Hatfield discusses previous Supreme Court cases to make his argument, but he can not propose a new case. (D) is incorrect since Hatfield opposes the addition of S. 815 to the constitutional amendment, saying that such an addition will "create question and raise confusion."

3. **(A)** This question requires that you select the type of evidence that Hatfield does NOT use. He does not make any reference to letters from students as he builds his argument. (B) is incorrect since he quotes two Supreme Court justices as well as a legal brief as evidence. (C) is incorrect; Hatfield uses the phrase "in my view" several times throughout his remarks. (D) is incorrect since Hatfield does use Supreme Court decisions as evidence for his position.

4. **(B)** Since the senator objects to prohibitions against students using public school buildings for prayer, he would support students' rights to organize a prayer club at a public high school. (A) is incorrect; the senator emphasizes that school prayer should be voluntary, not state-sponsored. (C) is incorrect; Senator Hatfield mention that he supports the right of students to gather for religious reasons using school facilities. (D) is incor-

rect; Hatfield would not support this activity since he argues that the Constitution "sets no limit on student-initiated prayer or religious discussion during noninstructional time periods."

5.   **(A)**   To find the most current debate over school prayer, a weekly news magazine like *Time* or *U.S. News & World Report* would be the best resource. (B) A religion textbook and (C) an encyclopedia would be useful for the background and history of school prayer in the U.S., but these sources might not be up-to-date. (D) Congressional records from the 1990s would be helpful for research on the legislative aspects of school prayer, but this choice is incorrect since these records would not cover the 2000s.

6.   **(C)**   is the correct answer; Senator Hatfield states emphatically that the first amendment guarantees this right. The test-taker should choose (C). (A) is incorrect; Senator Hatfield proposed Senate bill 815 himself and made his objections to the school prayer amendment. (B) is incorrect; Hatfield opposes adamantly the idea of including equal access language in a constitutional amendment. (D) is a wrong answer. Senator Hatfield says that elementary students have the same right to meet voluntarily during non-instructional time for prayer as do the secondary students. The test-taker should not choose (D).

7.   **(A)**   is the correct answer; the phrase "abdication of governmental institutions to the norm of secular humanism" means the giving up or abandonment of the institutions to anti-religious secular humanism. (B) is incorrect; the phrase implies that government showed no hostility or resistance to secular humanism. (C) is incorrect; "taking away or kidnapping" is actually the meaning of "abduction," not "abdication." (D) is a wrong answer; the implication of complete abandonment is much stronger than sensitivity.

8.   **(B)**   is the correct answer; Senator Hatfield goes on to say that these people "ought to realize that they are also raising some serious questions and confusion." Since creating confusion is not generally considered admirable, (A) is incorrect. (C) is incorrect; Hatfield does not believe they are harmless, but that they are causing trouble, however well-intentioned they may be. (D) is a wrong answer. Senator Hatfield says that those in question "ought to realize" the trouble they are causing, implying that he does not think they mean any harm.

9.   **(C)**   is the correct answer; Senator Hatfield states that what he did by proposing Senate bill 815 was to apply the right affirmed for public

university students to secondary school students as well. (A) is incorrect; if he thought the right were unnecessary, he probably would not have sought to extend it to more people. (B) is incorrect; if Hatfield thought it would lead to future problems, he probably would not have sought its extension. (D) is a wrong answer. Senator Hatfield says throughout the passage that the First Amendment guarantees this right, and thus he cannot be said to think it unconstitutional.

10. **(A)** is the correct answer; Senator Hatfield argues against the school prayer amendment and proposes an alternative. (B) is incorrect; Senator Hatfield argues against the school prayer amendment. (C) is incorrect; Hatfield mentions that the Supreme Court upheld the rights of public university students to use school facilities for religious purposes. (D) may be a true statement, but it is too narrow in its scope to represent the central idea of the passage.

11. Once you have written your response to this open-ended question, compare your answer with the two sample responses below. The good response (representing a score of 3 or 4) describes TWO strategies and provides clear explanations and examples of why the strategies are/are not effective that go "beyond the lines" of the text. The poor response (representing a score of 1 or 2) presents TWO strategies, but gives an example and slight explanation for only one strategy.

GOOD RESPONSE

One strategy Senator Hatfield uses is the strategy of quoting from experts to make his case persuasive. Senator Hatfield quotes Justices Black and Stewart, who represent two opposed views. Hatfield goes on to propose an alternative view. He uses quotes to build off of; he doesn't just choose quotes that support him. Hatfield's strategy works because he sets up the prior positions with quotes and then shows his alternative plan.

Another strategy used to great effectiveness by the senator is that of preemptively defending himself against likely criticism. As he states, the Supreme Court's decision that removed prayer from the classroom has been blamed for the decay in moral principles. Thus, he has surmised that if he is seen to support this decision, he will also be seen to be contributing to the decay in moral values. He avoids this criticism by mentioning his support for another Supreme Court decision that affirmed the right of public university students to use school facilities for religious purposes. Thus, he proves himself not to be an enemy of religion.

Senator Hatfield focuses mostly on providing hard facts for his argument, but they are facts guided by strategy.

POOR RESPONSE

Senator Hatfield tries to convince the reader by using persuasive language. This language is necessary for persuasive texts. He talks about Supreme Court cases. These are good to talk about because they decide things. So you can show what was decided and prove your argument that way. For example, he talks about the one where the university students wanted to pray, but the university didn't want to let them, and then the students sued them and they won.

12. Once you have written your response to this open-ended question, compare your answer with the two sample responses below. The good response (representing a score of 3 or 4) answers the question—both parts of it; it also includes an introduction and a conclusion. The poor response (representing a score of 1 or 0) presents a misunderstanding of the passage and contains many errors in spelling and usage.

GOOD RESPONSE

Senator Hatfield strikes a careful balance in his positions on school prayer. From his remarks about the proposed amendment, one can see the way in which he feels the students should and should not be permitted to conduct their prayer meeting.

Senator Hatfield stresses that prayer should be a right of students during noninstructional time. Groups can assemble in public buildings for prayer as well as for debates, chorus, etc. Hatfield suggests that administrators must allow voluntary meetings of students. He suggests that nondisruptive prayers are legal; not allowing such prayers violates the freedom of students and of groups. He also suggests that the constitutional right of university students belongs also to high school students. High school students should have the right to meet voluntarily on school property for religious purposes during noninstructional times.

Hatfield would also be opposed to the activity under certain circumstances. He mentions that the First Amendment limits the ability of government to "promote, establish, and inculcate" religious beliefs. Therefore, if the students wanted to have their prayer session endorsed or promoted by the school itself, Hatfield would oppose it.

Senator Hatfield does not wish to banish religious thought entirely from public schools. However, he does feel that it needs to be kept within certain limits to avoid infringing on students' freedom.

POOR RESPONSE

It would be very hard to find a way to have school prayer the way Hatfield wants it. He wants it not to be in instructional or noninstructional periods. It will be hard for the students to find a way to do it that will make him happy.

Hatfield opposes prayer in school in any form. So if the students want to do it even if the teacher says it is OK then he will try to stop it.

When I was in elementary school, we had prayer. Later we had silent meditation. I think either is fine. I agree that prayer is important.

I agree with prayer in school.

<u>Writing: revise/edit</u>

Below is a revised version of the student essay. Students taking the HSPA are not required to rewrite the essay, but space will be provided if they choose to do so instead of marking up the original.

The environment is something that I worry about. It hits me the most when instead of trees or plants in fields I see huge industrial plants. It amazes me how much smoke comes out of these huge monsters.

Not that I'm the best environmentalist. While I do recycle glass and aluminum cans, and I make sure to turn off lights and appliances, there are times that I'm too lazy to be active in saving the earth. I think of all the people like me who don't care if they throw garbage anywhere or if they waste water. I try to imagine how it all adds up, and the picture is over-whelming.

Yet that doesn't seem like it would even compare to things like cutting down the rain forests or destroying the ozone layer. There are so many species of animal life that we will never even see because of these devastations. Worse things seem to happen every day. Yet these things seem so far away from me that it's very hard to imagine.

I guess that someday these personal and industrial offenses to our world will add up against us. We seem to be ruining our world. What would it be like without clean air and grass? I imagine it would be like acid rain falling on a lot of metal.

NEW JERSEY

HSPA

High School Proficiency Assessment in

Language Arts

Practice
Test 2

HSPA
Language Arts

Practice Test 2
(See page 179 for answer sheets.)

TIME: Total Testing Time – Approximately 3 hours
Approximate section timing is as follows:
30 minutes for Writing: Speculate (picture prompt)
50 minutes for Reading: Narrative
60 minutes for Writing: Persuade
45 minutes for Reading: Persuasive
25 minutes for Writing: Revise/Edit

Note: The test is given over a two- or three-day period. Testing times and section lengths are approximate, and will vary from administration to administration.

Writing: speculate (picture prompt) – 30 mins.

Reprinted, by permission, from *The New York Times Magazine*, 5 August 2001, p. 39. Photograph by Lloyd De Grane.

Writing Task:

Look carefully at the photograph on the previous page. How would you characterize this scene? What does looking at this photo make you think or feel? Write an essay in which you imagine what kind of "story" might accompany this picture.

Reading (narrative) – 50 mins.

Introduction: In the following 1904 story by Jack London, the main character has to struggle for respect. Feel free to make marginal notes and/or underline as you read the text and answer the test questions.

THE STORY OF KEESH

KEESH lived long ago on the rim of the polar sea, was head man of his village through many and prosperous years, and died full of honors with his name on the lips of men. So long ago did he live that only the old men remember his name, his name and the tale, which they got from the old men before them, and which the old men to come will tell to their children and their children's children down to the end of time. And the winter darkness, when the north gales make their long sweep across the ice-pack, and the air is filled with flying white, and no man may venture forth, is the chosen time for the telling of how Keesh, from the poorest IGLOO in the village, rose to power and place over them all.

He was a bright boy, so the tale runs, healthy and strong, and he had seen thirteen suns, in their way of reckoning time. For each winter the sun leaves the land in darkness, and the next year a new sun returns so that they may be warm again and look upon one another's faces. The father of Keesh had been a very brave man, but he had met his death in a time of famine, when he sought to save the lives of his people by taking the life of a great polar bear. In his eagerness he came to close grapples with the bear, and his bones were crushed; but the bear had much meat on him and the people were saved. Keesh was his only son, and after that Keesh lived alone with his mother. But the people are prone to forget, and they forgot the deed of his father; and he being but a boy, and his mother only a woman, they, too, were swiftly forgotten, and ere long came to live in the meanest of all the IGLOOS.

It was at a council, one night, in the big IGLOO of Klosh-Kwan, the chief, that Keesh showed the blood that ran in his veins and the manhood that stiffened his back. With the dignity of an elder, he rose to his feet, and waited for silence amid the babble of voices.

"It is true that meat be apportioned me and mine," he said. "But it is ofttimes old and tough, this meat, and, moreover, it has an unusual quantity of bones."

The hunters, grizzled and gray, and lusty and young, were aghast. The like had never been known before. A child, that talked like a grown man, and said harsh things to their very faces!

But steadily and with seriousness, Keesh went on. "For that I know my father, Bok, was a great hunter, I speak these words. It is said that Bok brought home more meat than any of the two best hunters, that with his own hands he attended to the division of it, that with his own eyes he saw to it that the least old woman and the last old man received fair share."

"Na! Na!" the men cried. "Put the child out!" "Send him off to bed!" "He is no man that he should talk to men and graybeards!"

He waited calmly till the uproar died down. "Thou hast a wife, Ugh-Gluk," he said, "and for her dost thou speak. And thou, too, Massuk, a mother also, and for them dost thou speak. My mother has no one, save me; wherefore I speak. As I say, though Bok be dead because he hunted over-keenly, it is just that I, who am his son, and that Ikeega, who is my mother and was his wife, should have meat in plenty so long as there be meat in plenty in the tribe. I, Keesh, the son of Bok, have spoken."

He sat down, his ears keenly alert to the flood of protest and indignation his words had created.

"That a boy should speak in council!" old Ugh-Gluk was mumbling.

"Shall the babes in arms tell us men the things we shall do?" Massuk demanded in a loud voice. "Am I a man that I should be made a mock by every child that cries for meat?"

The anger boiled a white heat. They ordered him to bed, threatened that he should have no meat at all, and promised him sore beatings for his presumption. Keesh's eyes began to flash, and the blood to pound darkly under his skin. In the midst of the abuse he sprang to his feet.

"Hear me, ye men!" he cried. "Never shall I speak in the council again, never again till the men come to me and say, 'It is well, Keesh, that thou shouldst speak, it is well and it is our wish.' Take this now, ye men, for my last word. Bok, my father, was a great hunter. I, too, his son, shall go and hunt the meat that I eat. And be it known, now, that the division of that which I kill shall be fair. And no widow nor weak one shall cry in the night because there is no meat, when the strong men are groaning in great pain for that they have eaten overmuch. And in the days to come there shall be shame upon the strong men who have eaten overmuch. I, Keesh, have said it!"

Jeers and scornful laughter followed him out of the IGLOO, but his jaw was set and he went his way, looking neither to right nor left.

The next day he went forth along the shore-line where the ice and the land met together. Those who saw him go noted that he carried his bow, with a goodly supply of bone-barbed arrows, and that across his shoulder was his father's big hunting-spear. And there was laughter, and much talk, at the event. It was an unprecedented occurrence. Never did boys of his tender age go forth to hunt, much less to hunt alone. Also were there shaking of heads and prophetic mutterings, and the women looked pityingly at Ikeega, and her face was grave and sad.

"He will be back ere long," they said cheeringly.

"Let him go; it will teach him a lesson," the hunters said. "And he will come back shortly, and he will be meek and soft of speech in the days to follow."

But a day passed, and a second, and on the third a wild gale blew, and there was no Keesh. Ikeega tore her hair and put soot of the seal-oil on her face in token of her grief; and the women assailed the men with bitter words in that they had mistreated the boy and sent him to his death; and the men made no answer, preparing to go in search of the body when the storm abated.

Early next morning, however, Keesh strode into the village. But he came not shamefacedly. Across his shoulders he bore a burden of fresh-killed meat. And there was importance in his step and arrogance in his speech.

"Go, ye men, with the dogs and sledges, and take my trail for the better part of a day's travel," he said. "There is much meat on the ice - a she-bear and two half-grown cubs."

Ikeega was overcome with joy, but he received her demonstrations in manlike fashion, saying: "Come, Ikeega, let us eat. And after that I shall sleep, for I am weary."

And he passed into their IGLOO and ate profoundly, and after that slept for twenty running hours.

There was much doubt at first, much doubt and discussion. The killing of a polar bear is very dangerous, but thrice dangerous is it, and three times thrice, to kill a mother bear with her cubs. The men could not bring themselves to believe that the boy Keesh, single-handed, had accomplished so great a marvel. But the women spoke of the fresh-killed meat he had brought on his back, and this was an overwhelming argument against their unbelief. So they finally departed, grumbling greatly that in all probability, if the thing were so, he had neglected to cut up the carcasses. Now in the north it is very necessary that this should be done as soon as a kill is made. If not, the meat freezes so solidly as to turn the edge of the sharpest knife, and a three-hundred-pound bear, frozen stiff, is no easy thing to put upon a sled and haul over the rough ice. But arrived at the spot, they found not only the kill, which they had doubted, but that Keesh had quartered the beasts in true hunter fashion, and removed the entrails.

Thus began the mystery of Keesh, a mystery that deepened and deepened with the passing of the days. His very next trip he killed a young bear, nearly full-grown, and on the trip following, a large male bear and his mate. He was ordinarily gone from three to four days, though it was nothing unusual for him to stay away a week at a time on the ice-field. Always he declined company on these expeditions, and the people marvelled. "How does he do it?" they demanded of one another. "Never does he take a dog with him, and dogs are of such great help, too."

"Why dost thou hunt only bear?" Klosh-Kwan once ventured to ask him.

And Keesh made fitting answer. "It is well known that there is more meat on the bear," he said.

But there was also talk of witchcraft in the village. "He hunts with evil spirits," some of the people contended, "wherefore his hunting is rewarded. How else can it be, save that he hunts with evil spirits?"

"Mayhap they be not evil, but good, these spirits," others said. "It is known that his father was a mighty hunter. May not his father hunt with him so that he may attain excellence and patience and understanding? Who knows?"

None the less, his success continued, and the less skilful hunters were often kept busy hauling in his meat. And in the division of it he was just. As his father had done before him, he saw to it that the least old woman and the last old man received a fair portion, keeping no more for himself than his needs required. And because of this, and of his merit as a hunter, he was looked upon with respect, and even awe; and there was talk of making him chief after old Klosh-Kwan. Because of the things he had done, they looked for him to appear again in the council, but he never came, and they were ashamed to ask.

"I am minded to build me an IGLOO," he said one day to Klosh-Kwan and a number of the hunters. "It shall be a large IGLOO, wherein Ikeega and I can dwell in comfort."

"Ay," they nodded gravely.

"But I have no time. My business is hunting, and it takes all my time. So it is but just that the men and women of the village who eat my meat should build me my IGLOO."

And the IGLOO was built accordingly, on a generous scale which exceeded even the dwelling of Klosh-Kwan. Keesh and his mother moved into it, and it was the first prosperity she had enjoyed since the death of Bok. Nor was material prosperity alone hers, for, because of her wonderful son and the position he had given her, she came to be looked upon as the first woman in all the village; and the women were given to visiting her, to asking her advice, and to quoting her wisdom when arguments arose among themselves or with the men.

But it was the mystery of Keesh's marvellous hunting that took chief place in all their minds. And one day Ugh-Gluk taxed him with witchcraft to his face.

"It is charged," Ugh-Gluk said ominously, "that thou dealest with evil spirits, wherefore thy hunting is rewarded."

"Is not the meat good?" Keesh made answer. "Has one in the village yet to fall sick from the eating of it? How dost thou know that witchcraft be concerned? Or dost thou guess, in the dark, merely because of the envy that consumes thee?"

And Ugh-Gluk withdrew discomfited, the women laughing at him as he walked away. But in the council one night, after long deliberation, it was determined to put spies on his track when he went forth to hunt, so that his methods might be learned. So, on his next trip, Bim and Bawn, two young men, and of hunters the craftiest, followed after him, taking care not to be seen. After five days they returned, their eyes bulging and their tongues a-tremble to tell what they had seen. The council was hastily called in Klosh-Kwan's dwelling, and Bim took up the tale.

"Brothers! As commanded, we journeyed on the trail of Keesh, and cunningly we journeyed, so that he might not know. And midway of the first day he picked up with a great he-bear. It was a very great bear."

"None greater," Bawn corroborated, and went on himself. "Yet was the bear not inclined to fight, for he turned away and made off slowly over the ice. This we saw from the rocks of the shore, and the bear came toward us, and after him came Keesh, very much unafraid. And he shouted harsh words after the bear, and waved his arms about, and made much noise. Then did the bear grow angry, and rise up on his hind legs, and growl. But Keesh walked right up to the bear."

"Ay," Bim continued the story. "Right up to the bear Keesh walked. And the bear took after him, and Keesh ran away. But as he ran he dropped a little round ball on the ice. And the bear stopped and smelled of it, then swallowed it up. And Keesh continued to run away and drop little round balls, and the bear continued to swallow them up."

Exclamations and cries of doubt were being made, and Ugh-Gluk expressed open unbelief.

"With our own eyes we saw it," Bim affirmed.

And Bawn - "Ay, with our own eyes. And this continued until the bear stood suddenly upright and cried aloud in pain, and thrashed his fore paws madly about. And Keesh continued to make off over the ice to a safe distance. But the bear gave him no notice, being occupied with the misfortune the little round balls had wrought within him."

"Ay, within him," Bim interrupted. "For he did claw at himself, and leap about over the ice like a playful puppy, save from the way he growled and squealed it was plain it was not play but pain. Never did I see such a sight!"

"Nay, never was such a sight seen," Bawn took up the strain. "And furthermore, it was such a large bear."

"Witchcraft," Ugh-Gluk suggested.

"I know not," Bawn replied. "I tell only of what my eyes beheld. And after a while the bear grew weak and tired, for he was very heavy and he had jumped about with exceeding violence, and he went off along the shore-ice, shaking his head slowly from side to side and sitting down ever and again to squeal and cry. And Keesh followed after the bear, and we followed after Keesh, and for that day and three days more we followed. The bear grew weak, and never ceased crying from his pain."

"It was a charm!" Ugh-Gluk exclaimed. "Surely it was a charm!"

"It may well be."

And Bim relieved Bawn. "The bear wandered, now this way and now that, doubling back and forth and crossing his trail in circles, so that at the end he was near where Keesh had first come upon him. By this time he was quite sick, the bear, and could crawl no farther, so Keesh came up close and speared him to death."

"And then?" Klosh-Kwan demanded.

"Then we left Keesh skinning the bear, and came running that the news of the killing might be told."

And in the afternoon of that day the women hauled in the meat of the bear while the men sat in council assembled. When Keesh arrived a messenger was sent to him, bidding him come to the council. But he sent reply, saying that he was hungry and tired; also that his IGLOO was large and comfortable and could hold many men.

And curiosity was so strong on the men that the whole council, Klosh-Kwan to the fore, rose up and went to the IGLOO of Keesh. He was eating, but he received them with respect and seated them according to their rank. Ikeega was proud and embarrassed by turns, but Keesh was quite composed.

Klosh-Kwan recited the information brought by Bim and Bawn, and at its close said in a stern voice: "So explanation is wanted, O Keesh, of thy manner of hunting. Is there witchcraft in it?"

Keesh looked up and smiled. "Nay, O Klosh-Kwan. It is not for a boy to know aught of witches, and of witches I know nothing. I have but devised a means whereby I may kill the ice-bear with ease, that is all. It be headcraft, not witchcraft."

"And may any man?"

"Any man."

There was a long silence. The men looked in one another's faces, and Keesh went on eating.

"And . . . and . . . and wilt thou tell us, O Keesh?" Klosh-Kwan finally asked in a tremulous voice.

"Yea, I will tell thee." Keesh finished sucking a marrow-bone and rose to his feet. "It is quite simple. Behold!"

He picked up a thin strip of whalebone and showed it to them. The ends were sharp as needle-points. The strip he coiled carefully, till it disappeared in his hand. Then, suddenly releasing it, it sprang straight again. He picked up a piece of blubber.

"So," he said, "one takes a small chunk of blubber, thus, and thus makes it hollow. Then into the hollow goes the whalebone, so, tightly coiled, and another piece of blubber is fitted over the whale-bone. After that it is put outside where it freezes into a little round ball. The bear swallows the little round ball, the blubber melts, the whalebone with its sharp ends stands out straight, the bear gets sick, and when the bear is very sick, why, you kill him with a spear. It is quite simple."

And Ugh-Gluk said "Oh!" and Klosh-Kwan said "Ah!" And each said something after his own manner, and all understood.

And this is the story of Keesh, who lived long ago on the rim of the polar sea. Because he exercised headcraft and not witchcraft, he rose from the meanest IGLOO to be head man of his village, and through all the years that he lived, it is related, his tribe was prosperous, and neither widow nor weak one cried aloud in the night because there was no meat.

1.   The story says that Bawn "corroborated" Bim's story. In this context, "corroborated" means

(A) exaggerated.

(B) confirmed.

(C) continued.

(D) contradicted.

2. According to the story, who was the chief and leader of the village when Keesh began to hunt?

   (A) Keesh

   (B) Keesh's father, Bok

   (C) Klosh

   (D) Klosh-Kwan

3. Overall, how did the elders respond to Keesh's challenging words?

   (A) They were surprised at his words, and were impressed.

   (B) They drew back in fear, and were frightened.

   (C) They laughed at him.

   (D) They thought he was being too bold, and were offended.

4. What did the people in Keesh's village suspect about Keesh?

   (A) That he hunted with evil spirits.

   (B) That he was a good hunter.

   (C) That he was stealing other hunters' kills.

   (D) That Keesh would not share the meat equally in the village.

5. What happened to Keesh's mother because of her son's success in hunting?

   (A) The villagers feared her.

   (B) She received greater respect and comfort.

   (C) People accused her of being a witch.

   (D) She became the new leader.

6. Why does Keesh not tell the elders about his hunting methods earlier?

   (A) He does not wish to share his success.

   (B) He fears they will laugh at his methods.

   (C) He wants them first to acknowledge him respectfully.

   (D) They are too old to use his method.

7. How did Keesh respond when Klosh-Kwan asks him if he used witchcraft?

    (A) He got angry.

    (B) He smiled.

    (C) He changed the subject.

    (D) He refused to answer.

8. In the villagers' way of reckoning time, "suns" equal

    (A) years.

    (B) days.

    (C) winters.

    (D) summers.

9. This story is MOSTLY about

    (A) How Keesh's father died.

    (B) How Keesh gained control of the group.

    (C) How Keesh learned the best way to hunt.

    (D) How the elders learned to respect Keesh.

10. After Keesh's first hunt, the men going out to collect the carcass figure that Keesh has failed to cut it up. The carcass had to be cut up because otherwise

    (A) wolves would eat the meat.

    (B) someone might steal the carcass.

    (C) the meat would freeze solid.

    (D) the meat would fall through the ice.

11. Pick one of the main characters (either Keesh or Klosh-Kwan) and discuss how the character changes during the story.

12. Describe the scene in which Bim and Bawn tell the elders what they saw when they followed Keesh on his hunt. Who is present during their story? What do they learn, and what does the reader learn, in this scene?

<u>Writing: persuade – 60 mins.</u>

<u>Directions for Writing:</u> Write an essay analyzing and evaluating these opposing views on the minimum wage. You may include personal experience, knowledge, or observations.

The minimum wage in America has been the subject of debate for many years. Many people argue we should be careful about sharp increases in the minimum wage because of the resulting inflation (higher labor costs equal higher consumer prices) and layoffs. Others believe the minimum wage is too low to support a family and should be raised to keep up with the cost of living.

<u>Reading: persuasive – 45 mins.</u>

Introduction: In the following essay by Suzanne Britt Jordan, the writer expresses her views on two different lifestyles. Feel free to make marginal notes and/or underline as you read the text and answer the test questions.

Adapted from "That Lean and Hungry Look"

You can take it from Julius Caesar: you've got to watch people. I've watched them for a long time, and it's not a pretty sight. I shake at lean men around me. You find all sorts of these "leanies" about if you look long enough: the condescending lean man, the "he's got it all together" lean man, the efficiency expert lean man — all lean, all a social nuisance.

Leanies are funless. They don't mess around in the fat way. Their messing leads somewhere, amounts to something, proves constructive in some way. That's not true messing. Five minutes with nothing to do but drink coffee will get you an empty cup, cleaned and washed and put back on the rack along with the coffee spoon spotless and in the drawer, the cream and sugar nowhere in sight. Full of industry as they are, leanies say things like, "I need a twenty-five-hour day to get everything done." Fat people consider the day too confounded long as it is.

Also, leanies are tiringly energetic to the point of being unhealthy. On "slow" they're in a dead run. There's always that executive briskness in their walk, as if they are always on their way to an important meeting with the board when all they're really headed for is the bathroom. They're always ready to "tackle" and "meet head-on." But fat people say, "Give me your sluggish, your inert, your 'give me a minute, will ya!' type who intelligently conclude: mop it today, they just track it up tomorrow."

Mostly, the leanies oppress. They always have good intentions. What happened to the nice, healthy attitude, "I wasn't gonna do it anyway"? Or they parade around with bony trunks, ship shapes, alert eyes, straight posture — the kind a mugger never hits in the parking lot. Their shirt tails are never out; they never sit back on the sofa, always on the edge. They always keep their left hands in their laps at lunch. Fat people keep it loose, comfortable, spread out, soft. They can fearlessly slouch to their cars in parking lots because crooks see immediately they probably spent all their money inside on popcorn and pizza. They don't keep their hands in their laps when they eat. That's where the napkin goes.

And leanies are stupidly logical. There's that condescending shake of the head before they start to tell you how stupid you are. There's the index finger that counts off on the other hand the list of things so you won't lose track. They know the TV schedule — those that even watch TV — when it comes to news programs, educational programs, and prerecorded exercise shows. They know about cholesterol and smoking, body fats, and safe sex. And always, always they are financially responsible and sound.

Fat people, on the other hand, are comfortably illogical — not stupid, you understand. But we tend to see the other side of "smart" and "with it." We don't know the TV schedule because we don't have a TV schedule. Not only that, but having a TV schedule implies planning ahead. Planning ahead to watch a show you watch each week whether you plan to or not somehow takes the fun out of it; it removes the spontaneity of life. And while fat people aren't into keeping up with their cholesterol or triglycerides, they are aware that chances are you'll die in a car accident before your arteries kill you.

1. Which of the following best defines "inert" in the third paragraph of this selection?

   (A) Unintelligent

   (B) Helpless

   (C) Ignored

   (D) Not active

2. Which of the following statements best expresses the main idea of paragraph two?

   (A) Fat people don't have a productive purpose in life.

   (B) Thin people can take any situation in life and convert it into a productive experience.

   (C) The approach that thin people have toward life is lifeless and boring because everything has to be productive.

(D) Thin people should learn how to mess around in a fat way.

3. Which of the following statements would the writer of the selection most likely agree with?

(A) Happy people are more likely to be fat people.

(B) Fat people will usually outlive thin people.

(C) Thin people aren't as successful as they appear.

(D) Happy people actually have more intelligence than thin people.

4. Which of the following, according to the selection, would best sum up the writer's point in the third paragraph about the "executive briskness" in the thin person's walk?

(A) Much of the energy of a thin person is "put on."

(B) Fat people don't know how to walk fast.

(C) Executives are more likely to be thin and energetic.

(D) Thin people are better workers.

5. Which of the following lists of topics best organizes information presented in the selection?

(A) I.   Ways thin people approach life

II. Ways fat people approach life

III. Superiority of the "fat" approach

(B) I.   Lean people are unsocial

II. Lean people are unhealthy

III. Lean people are stupid

(C) I.   Lessons that lean people could learn from fat people

II. How to conserve energy

III. How to stay healthy

IV. How to view life

(D) I.   Problems with thin people

II. A perspective of fat people.

6. The word "oppress" as it is used in paragraph 4 means

   (A) to exercise authority over someone.

   (B) to annoy.

   (C) to assist.

   (D) to lead by example.

7. The satirical message of the passage is most likely a response to

   (A) the likelihood of dying in a car accident.

   (B) the belief of the leanies that they are better than others.

   (C) society's prejudice against people with weight problems.

   (D) the pressure to succeed in the modern world.

8. The two phrases "Leanies are stupidly logical...Fat people, on the other hand, are comfortably illogical" form an example of

   (A) exaggeration.

   (B) comparison.

   (C) contrast.

   (D) hyperbole.

9. The writer's attitude towards the "leanies" could best be described as

   (A) hostile.

   (B) sympathetic.

   (C) superior.

   (D) jealous.

10. The writer's use of the words "fat" and "lean" could best be described as

   (A) literal.

   (B) symbolic.

   (C) sarcastic.

   (D) exaggerated.

DIRECTIONS: For questions 11 and 12, write your answer in the space provided in the back of the book, referring to the passage "That Lean and Hungry Look." Address all parts of the question.

11. How do you think leanies might respond to this passage?

   • Refer to the way leanies are described in the passsage to theorize about their likely reactions.

12. What does the writer mean when she refers to leanies with the oxymoron "stupidly logical"?

   • Cite at least two examples given in the text to which this description might apply

Writing: revise/edit – 25 mins.

Karen is writing to her principal to see if it is possible to get e-mail accounts for her high school. She has asked you to review her letter before she hands it in. Feel free to make marks in the text as you read, revise, and edit. Alternatively, you may rewrite the essay to include your corrections.

Dear Principal Thomason:

I'm writing to suggest an addition to the computer program in our school. Since computers are quickly becoming an important part of our society, I believe that our students should have an understanding of computers that goes beyond word processing. In addition to more computers, it would be very beneficial if we could have access to the Internet. By giving students accounts that would provide access to e-mail and the Internet, the school will provide its students with many opportunities in the future.

The "Information Superhighway" is becoming more and more popular across the nation. The Internet connects millions of computers together to share information about a variety of subjects. Because computers are necessary to survive in the business world, it is important for the students in our school to learn these skills. These accounts would give us this experience firsthand, so we would not have to learn about it in a book. We would be more markitable to our employers, which would in turn be a positive reflection on our school.

Access to the Internet would improve our work within school. Using computers, we could learn about the subjects we study in new ways. The Internet offers endless amounts of information about everything. While we were learning computer skills, we would also be learning things for our other classes. It would put a whole new meaning into our book reports!

We could also talk to other people on the Internet about what we are studying. This access would introduce us to new people and experiences we otherwise might not never know. This communication is similar to writing a letter just travel more quickly, and there is no cost for postage! People can now communicates with others around the world by typing messages on a computer. People can also play games on the computer.

To have access to the Internet on our own is very expensive. It requires a computer and you also need an account to access the Internet. These accounts are arrange through services which can be very expensive. Since most of the colleges we students will be going on to will not only provide but require computer usage, I think our school should do the same.

Thank you for your consideration.

HSPA
PRACTICE TEST 2

ANSWER KEY

Reading: narrative

1.	(B)	6.	(C)	11.	Essay
2.	(D)	7.	(B)	12.	Essay
3.	(D)	8.	(A)		
4.	(A)	9.	(D)		
5.	(B)	10.	(C)		

Reading: persuasive

1.	(D)	6.	(A)	11.	Essay
2.	(C)	7.	(B)	12.	Essay
3.	(A)	8.	(C)		
4.	(A)	9.	(C)		
5.	(D)	10.	(B)		

DETAILED EXPLANATIONS OF ANSWERS

HSPA LANGUAGE ARTS

TEST 2

Writing: speculate (picture prompt)

GOOD RESPONSE

Pedro squinted at the tiny electronic readout. It was strong, and it was leading him somewhere. He had to stop occasionally to let the machine settle down—apparently he was so close that the computer was going wild with excitement.

"Are you getting this, Pedro? My readings are so off the scale I think my machine is malfunctioning." So said Pedro's friend Juanita. Juanita was a good person to have along on these hunts, but Pedro wished that she wouldn't bring her little brother Armando along. All that kid ever seemed to do was climb all over everything in sight and try to make a nuisance of himself.

"I think your machine is fine, Juanita. Mine is going loco too. Come on down this way—I can see that we've got competition." Pedro could tell that the boy across the sidewalk had a machine like his, and there was no doubt that he was hot on the trail too.

But Pedro was faster, and better with his machine too. He raced down a back alley, with Juanita and Armando right behind. His machine's frenzied beeping led him to an enormous and very filthy dumpster.

"Don't tell me it's in that," sneered Armando.

"Only one way to find out," said Pedro. He got Juanita to help him up, and disappeared under the dumpster's lid.

Ten seconds passed, then twenty. Juanita and Armando looked at each other nervously. Then at last Pedro's head popped out of the massive bin, with a great smile. "It's here all right—more of it than I've ever seen!"

Pedro raised his right hand; it was full of a dark green vine. Juanita and Armando recognized it as the Francisco vine—the plant with remarkable healing powers that grew as a weed. None of them knew why it was so common in their neighborhood's garden lately, but they knew what it could do, and how valuable it was.

Pedro raised himself and sprang out of the dumpster. He and his friends took the vine to a local doctor, who paid them handsomely. Then the group took out their little machines and waited for the next sign of the Francisco vine to appear.

Features of the Good Response

This story is clear and well organized. There are no obvious mechanical errors and the sentences smoothly build on each other. There is a sense of focus, and that the ideas evolve naturally. The author is attentive to detail, but is sure to use some imaginative conjecture when interpreting the "narrative" of this photograph.

POOR RESPONSE

The kids are hanging out. There are four kids. They hang out on the corner to play video games. With each other. One is wearing a red shirt and the other is wearing a yellow on and the little kid has a cap on and the girl also has red on. These are the four kids. Their is a fire hydrant, a stop sign, and a store with signs in Spanish. The sidewalk looks kind of dirty. They might be in Mexico. Maybe not though. It looks like there is a pay phone in the background. And a women, who is carrying something in her hands. The kids all have video games. Video games are fun. They used to be ones you had to play on your TV set, but now everyone has the kind you can walk around with. Some adults even play these kind, on the bus or when they are at home. Lots of kids I know play these kinds of games because they are fun. And you can take them with you. The smallest kid's pants are too big for him.

Features of the Poor Response

This essay is poorly organized. There are several usage and mechanical errors, including sentence fragments, run-on sentences, and an incorrect use of "Their" instead of "There" in the seventh sentence. The author describes the photo and offers many details about it, but does not expand on them creatively. The digression about video games distracts from talking about the photo, and the last sentence is clearly out of place—it should come when the author is describing the way the children are dressed. The author is also incorrect about some details—the kids aren't all playing games (the boy on the hydrant isn't, for instance).

Reading (narrative)

1. **(B)** Bawn witnessed the same events as Bim and can thus confirm that his story is true. Though he does continue (C) the tale, this is not the meaning of "corroborated." Contradiction (D) would imply that Bawn said something different than Bim, but they agree on the facts.

2. **(D)** Although Keesh became the chief when he became a fully grown man, when the story opens the chief is named Klosh-Kwan. Keesh's father Bok (B) is mentioned as a "brave man" but not as the chief.

3. **(D)** While it is true that the elders were surprised at Keesh's words, they were mostly offended. They did not fear him (B), for he was just a boy. They were too offended to take it lightly and laugh (C).

4. **(A)** Because no one in the village had ever seen such a successful hunter as Keesh, they assumed he was getting assistance from supernatural forces. The elders thought it impossible that he should be such a good hunter (A). Thievery (C) is not mentioned; from the beginning of his hunting, Keesh shared equally, which eliminates (D).

5. **(B)** Keesh's mother has a larger igloo than before, and the other women of the village come to her for advice. People think that her son may be using witchcraft, but no one accuses her of being a witch (C). She does not become the leader (D), as it remains Klosh-Kwan.

6. **(C)** In his first conversation with the elders, Keesh concludes by saying that he will not speak to the council again until they come to him and say it is well that he should speak. This happens at the story's end, and Keesh answers their questions once they give him this respect. He is willing to share his secret, disproving (A). He is too confident to fear laughter (B), and he says that any man may use his secret, disproving (D).

7. **(B)** Keesh was not offended when he was asked this question. It seemed to amuse him. He did not change the subject (C) or refuse to

answer (D), but went into detail about how his methods were not witch-craft but "headcraft."

8.   **(A)**   As explained in the first paragraph, a "sun" represents the time of an entire cycle of seasons, i.e. a year, as the sun is "born" in the warm season and "dies" again in the dark winter. Keesh is thirteen suns, or thirteen years, old as the story begins. Winter (C) and summer (D) are incorrect, as the term refers to the entire cycle of seasons.

9.   **(D)**   The story tells very little about how Keesh's father died. Though it is mentioned that Keesh became the "head man" in his village, his gaining control is not the main focus. The story also says only a little about how Keesh learned to hunt the way that he did. However, a great deal of emphasis is put on the way Keesh wins over the elders by his hunting methods.

10. **(C)**   Wolves are never mentioned in the story. Likewise, thieves and objects falling through the ice are not concerns; (C) is the only one cited in the story.

11. Once you have written your response to this open-ended question, compare your answer with the two sample responses below. The good response (representing a score of 3 or 4) offers several pieces of evidence to support the writer's conclusion, and has clear organization of its information. The poor response (representing a score of 1 or 0) offers almost no evidence and distractingly offers irrelevant opinions.

GOOD RESPONSE

Klosh-Kwan, along with the other characters in this story, learns not only to take Keesh seriously as a good hunter, but perhaps also to look past appearances. They thought that Keesh, because he was so young, would have nothing to offer the village, and therefore did not have to be considered. What he and the others learned is that a new idea can change the world; the collective lives of the village were definitely changed, because they no longer had to worry about having enough food. Chances are pretty good that the next time someone says that they will do something, even something that seems unlikely, that the Chief and the other elders will think, "maybe it is possible. After all, look at what Keesh managed to do." This is an important change, and it can happen in any community.

POOR RESPONSE

Keesh didn't change at all he knew what he wanted and went and got it. This is ridiculous! There's no change. I guess he had an idea, and people treated him different, but really he didn't change. I like the part where he stood up for himself.

12. Once you have written your response to this open-ended question, compare your answer with the two sample responses below. The good response (representing a score of 3 or 4) offers four pieces of evidence to support the writer's conclusion, and has clear organization of its information. The poor response (representing a score of 1 or 0) offers almost no evidence and distractingly offers details about the writer's own life.

GOOD RESPONSE

The chief sends two hunters, Bim and Bawn, out to follow Keesh and see how he is able to kill all of the polar bears that he is bringing back to the village. They are gone for a long time, and when they come back they seem terrified! This is because they saw Keesh do something amazing while hunting, and the two story-tellers cannot understand how he did it. They describe what they saw in great detail, taking turns each of them. They watched Keesh stalk a very large polar bear, and then toss out little round balls of something, which the bear ate. Then they tell how the bear acted very strangely, as if playful yet in obvious pain, until it was so weak it could barely move. Then Keesh killed it.

The elders are shocked to hear this story. They are alarmed, even Klosh-Kwan, the chief. They assume that Keesh is using the help of evil spirits, which is what they suspected all along. Though they don't actually come out and say it, they are afraid. Ugh-Gluk especially is disturbed; he is the one who had publicly questioned Keesh on the way that the hunter had been having success while hunting. At the end of the scene, they hear that Keesh has returned to camp. When the messenger they send to Keesh comes back saying that Keesh is too tired to see them, they all go to Keesh's igloo, to find out from him the method he has been using to hunt.

POOR RESPONSE

The two hunters come back and they are very nervous. When they tell their story all the other guys get nervous too. The story goes that they watched Keesh kill a bear by feeding it balls of something the bear acts funny and then he spears it. They came running back. The other men act all concerned, and say that Keesh is evil. When he comes back, they go to talk to him and maybe kick him out of town or something.

Writing: persuade

GOOD RESPONSE

There is no doubt that minimum wage laws are necessary for the well-being of workers and their families. It had always been the policy for most businesses to pay laborers less than they deserve. Minimum wage laws are one of the only ways workers can be protected from management; without them they are fair game to whatever exploitation the employer can manage.

Many argue against the minimum wage, protesting that it is too high. The fact is, even with raises in the rate, it still does not meet the needs of the laborers because of the increases in inflation and the basic cost of living. At present, it would be extremely difficult, or even impossible, to support a family on a salary as low as $5.15 an hour. There is no person (or family) in my experience who survives on minimum wages; teenagers, who have financial help from their parents, might find a minimum wage adequate, but no "head of a household" would. If anything, the current minimum wage rate is too low.

Another argument against minimum wage, especially sharp increases, is the possibility of inflation due to higher labor costs which might cause higher consumer prices. The problem with this is management. Workers do not cause inflation, businesses and corporations do. If the leaders of these companies were not so money hungry, workers could have higher salaries without causing an increase in the price of goods and services. It is quite possible to do this because products are extremely overpriced. Most businesses, however, look to short-term, easy money instead of long term stability. A raise in the minimum wage would actually help the business in the long run because workers would be happier and thus, productivity would be increased. The only way a raise in the minimum wage would cause inflation would be if the companies themselves let it.

The final point made by those opposed to minimum wage is the possibility of inflationary pressures resulting in worker lay-offs. As was discussed earlier, inflation in this situation is not a given. For the moment however, let's just theorize on the possibilities of workers being fired. Those most likely to be laid off are the teenagers, minorities, seniors, and the disabled. Although this seems like the course of action many businesses would take, it is not if the companies are smart. First, firing workers would not be tolerated by unions. Next, even in non-union companies, laying off workers would cost the business money in the long run; with less workers, productivity is diminished and when there is a need for more workers they will have to be paid at the same wage as were the ones who were fired. There is little chance that businesses would make decisions that would cost them money.

It would be ridiculous to say that minimum wage is a panacea for the laborers of the world. It barely makes a dent, especially with the recent increases in their bills. What it does do, though, is give the worker a guarantee that he will get paid no less than is mandated; this, in many cases, is enough.

Features of the Good Response

This essay is thoughtful and well-organized, introducing several interesting arguments supporting the minimum wage. The author obviously has some knowledge and experience about the effect of minimum wage legislation on businesses and tries to debunk arguments that a minimum wage necessarily means inflation, higher costs, and layoffs. The writer presents his/her views straightforwardly and clearly, although the opinions expressed may not be popular (or accurate) from an employer's point of view.

Still, the author systematically addresses the most typical arguments against the minimum wage and reaches a realistic conclusion. In other words, he/she doesn't argue that minimum wage is a panacea, but merely a help. In addition, the syntax is quite readable, there are few errors of any kind, and the text is easy to follow. The essay is very well-developed considering the writing time allotted.

POOR RESPONSE

The baby begins to cry as the father enters the run-down apartment. He dodges the dripping ceiling and proceeds over to help his wife who is caught between the bargain dinner and the crying child. After soothes the child he goes onto explain that on account of his low wage, there will not be any hot water for a while. We can't have everything, it was either that or the streets.

I don't believe that the minimum wage is higher. It is not fair, some people should be expected to live such a low standard. The Adult work force should be given a more fair and reliable wage to support themselves. Then they would gain a better self esteem and, in turn, give their children a better outlook on life.

The minimum wage does not have to be raised for the teenagers. I believe there should be separate minimums for minors and adults. This way a business owner does not have to pay extra for a teenagers incompetence, and the adult worker who is struggling to support a family is much better.

The poverty levels of this country is increasing more and more. If the minimum wages would be lifted for adults it may aliviate some of the poverty. It may also solve some problems for many struggling families who are going homeless, and once your homeless, the minimum wage doesn't matter any more.

Features of the Poor Response

This essay begins with a rather interesting and compelling vignette describing the effects of a "non-living" wage. Unfortunately, this is the only real positive aspect of the essay.

There are several errors in punctuation and syntax. A good example is the comma splice in the first paragraph: "We can't have everything, it was either that or the streets." The author does however, take a clear stand on the issue of the minimum wage, and presents an alternative solution to the problem. He/she suggests that teenagers be paid a lower minimum wage than adults, but fails to explore the potential difficulties with such a proposal.

The essay concludes with a grim reminder of the effects of insufficient pay—poverty and homelessness—and ends the essay where it began. Though the writer clearly has a sense of style, the essay loses its power due to its inadequate development and frequent writing errors.

Reading: persuasive

1.   **(D)**   The word "sluggish" provides a key clue. (A) is incorrect; the sentence containing the word has nothing to do with intelligence. (B) is incorrect; the writer is not referring to those who can't help themselves but to those who don't care to act. (C) is incorrect; the writer's concern is not with those who receive no attention. Generally, only (D) reflects the context clue given in the paragraph.

2.   **(C)**   Sentence one contains this idea as a topic concept while the rest of the paragraph shows how dull the "thin" approach is and how different it is from the "fat" approach. (A) is incorrect; the writer neither says nor implies such a conclusion. (B) is incorrect; while this statement may be true, it misses the writer's intent: the productive approach is "funless," dull. (D) is incorrect; the writer may think this, but she doesn't say it and her intent is not to say what thin people should do but what they actually do (or do not do).

3. **(A)** When the author asserts that thin people are funless, she in essence agrees with this; the entire selection implies it clearly. (B) is incorrect; the writer in no way tries to argue that fat people live longer, just happier. (C) is incorrect; if anything, she thinks they are every bit as successful as they appear. (D) is incorrect; she doesn't argue about intelligence in the selection.

4. **(A)** According to the context, the thin person walks as if to convey executive urgency when in fact the situation is otherwise. (B) is incorrect; the writer might say this humorously, but the point is not a fat person's walking speed. (C) is incorrect; the writer implies that brisk walkers are not true executives. (D) is incorrect; if anything, the opposite here would be true, although the point isn't whether thin people are good or poor in their performance.

5. **(D)** Paragraphs two through five discuss a different aspect of life as leanies see it; the final sentence alludes to the fat counterperspective. Paragraph four addresses the fat viewpoint in slightly more depth. Paragraph six then looks at the fat viewpoint. (A) is incorrect; the selection doesn't focus on the ways fat people approach life but on the ways lean people approach it. (B) is incorrect; although the three key words in the answer may appear in the selection, they do not reflect the main ideas of the respective paragraphs. (C) is incorrect; the point of the selection is not to teach lessons to lean people; the paragraphs' intentions are not to do such things as teach how to conserve energy or to stay healthy.

6. **(A)** The passage refers to the leanies subtly trying to enforce their will on others, confident that their way is best; this is the meaning of "oppress" as used in the passage. (B) is incorrect; the leanies may well annoy other people, but this is not the meaning of the word. (C) is incorrect; the leanies may think they are assisting people, but their help is unwanted and unwarranted. (D) is incorrect; again, the leanies may believe they are doing this, but the passage is not written from their perspective.

7. **(B)** The writer makes it clear that what really annoys her, and why she is writing, is that the leanies always think they know what is best. (A) is incorrect; the writer does mention this, but it does not appear that she is overly concerned with it. (C) is incorrect; the writer does not address the attitudes of society in general, but only the leanies versus the fat people. (D) is incorrect; the writer does not mention such pressure.

8. **(C)** This is an example of contrast because it shows the differences between the two approaches. (A) is incorrect; the quoted section does not make things out to be more than they are. (B) is incorrect; the quoted section does not show how the two approaches are similar, but how they are different. (D) is incorrect; the quoted material does not employ extreme, exaggerated language.

9. **(C)** The writer is confident that her approach to life is better than that of the misguided leanies. (A) is incorrect; the writer does not seem to want harm to befall the leanies. (B) is incorrect; the writer does seem to understand the position of the leanies, but she disagrees with it too much to be called sensitive. (D) is incorrect; the author does not want to be like the leanies, for she believes they are misguided.

10. **(B)** is the best answer; the writer uses the terms to signify not so much physical shapes but approaches to life. (A) is incorrect; as mentioned, the writer uses the terms to mean something other than their literal significance. (C) is incorrect; it would mean that the writer means the opposite of what she says, and this is not true. (D) is incorrect; the writer is not exaggerating people's fatness of leanness, but using it to symbolize their approaches to life.

11. Once you have written your response to this open-ended question, compare your work with the two sample responses below. Notice that the good response (representing a score of 3 or 4) discusses THREE well-explained conclusions with good support from the text. The poor response (representing a score of 1 or 0) is awkwardly organized and presents ONE conclusion with an unclear, oversimplified explanation that features little support from the text.

GOOD RESPONSE

The response of a leanie to this passage would most likely be one of frustration. The leanie would see that all good intentions have been wasted on this writer; he would be shocked that she even had the gall to claim she had the right ideas about life; ultimately, though, he would probably ignore her.

The fifth paragraph mentions how the leanie will shake his head before carefully counting off the ways in which the fat person is stupid. As annoying as this may be to the fat person, it is clear by his condescending attitude that the leanie really thinks he is doing the fat person a service. The leanie would probably give another condescending shake of his head when the author aligns herself with the fat, lazy people. It would be clear to him that he or his fellow leanies have been wasting their time with this woman, and wasting time is something they hate.

The leanie would also be shocked by the nerve of this writer. She describes his people, who consider themselves to know what is best for everyone, as "stupidly logical." She even downplays his importance by suggesting that he is really just on the way to the bathroom when he is making his brisk trot through the office, looking determined.

Finally, though, the leanie would not spend too much time reacting to the passage. Leanies are efficiency experts and people who need "twenty-five hour days" to get everything done. A leanie would probably see fairly quickly that this woman is too stubborn to be "helped" and would therefore move on to something more productive.

POOR RESPONSE

The leanie would get very angry at the passage. The writer calls him stupid. I would get mad if somebody called me stupid. I think the writer is being mean. She is lazy and she wants other people to be lazy like her. The leanie people just want to help. You just can't help somebody who doesn't want to be helped though like this woman. She is too set in her ways. Probably she is too old to change. People get like that when they get old.

12. Once you have written your response to this open-ended question, compare your work with the two sample responses below. Notice that the good response (representing a score of 3 or 4) discusses TWO well-explained points with good support from the text. The poor response (representing a score of 1 or 2) presents TWO points but explains them poorly (in a way that shows a lack of full understanding of the question) and features little support from the text.

GOOD RESPONSE

The writer describes leanies as "stupidly logical" because, while they might appear to be doing things in a logical and efficient manner, the things they are doing are often themselves illogical. They are logical in the details but miss the point of the "big picture." This can be easily seen in their approaches to such everyday activities as drinking coffee and watching television.

The writer describes how a leanie given five minutes with nothing to do but drink coffee will end his five minutes with the coffee cup empty and all the condiments put away. The writer does not consider this to be the point of sitting down for a cup of coffee; as she puts it, "that's not true messing." The leanie, because of his insatiable urge for efficiency and productivity, has missed out on the pleasure of sitting down and leisurely sipping a good cup of coffee.

The leanie can even turn that paragon of leisure, the television, into a vehicle for efficiency. As the fifth paragraph reveals, those leanies that do watch television know the schedule ahead of time so they can watch their news, educational programs, and exercise shows. However, as the final paragraph shows, the lean approach defies the point of watching television. She complains that the lean way takes the fun out of it and removes the spontaneity. One can see that she considers television to be for relaxation and pleasure, and to make it regimented and planned is antithetical to that purpose.

As is revealed by their approaches to everyday activities, the leanies are too worried about efficiency to stop and focus on the real point of life—which, for this writer, is to enjoy it.

POOR RESPONSE

Leanies just don't get it. I know what the writer was talking about. They are stupidly logical because logic is stupid. The world is crazy and you just have to enjoy it if you can. They keep their hands in their laps at lunch. This is stupid logic because it is much easier to eat when you use both hands.

Another way in which they use stupid logic is when they watch TV. They watch only the boring shows, the ones that try to teach you something. There's nothing wrong with learning, but that's not what TV is for, in my opinion. You shouldn't be learning anything when watching TV. It's just for fun and for nothing else.

Writing: revise/edit

Below is a revised version of the student essay. Students taking the HSPA are not required to rewrite the essay, but space will be provided if they choose to do so instead of marking up the original.

Dear Principal Thomason:

I'm writing to suggest an addition to the computer program in our school. Since computers are quickly becoming an important part of our society, I believe that our students should have an understanding of computers that goes beyond word processing. In addition to more computers, it would be very beneficial if we could have access to the Internet. By giving students accounts that would provide access to e-mail and the Internet, the school will provide its students with many opportunities in the future.

The "Information Superhighway" is becoming more and more popular across the nation. The Internet connects millions of computers together to share information about a variety of subjects. Because computers are necessary to survive in the business world, it is important for the students in our school to learn these skills. These accounts would give us this experience firsthand, so we would not have to learn about it in a book. We would be more marketable to our employers, which would in turn be a positive reflection on our school.

Access to the Internet would improve our work within school. Using computers, we could learn about the subjects we study in new ways. The Internet offers endless amounts of information about everything. While we were learning computer skills, we would also be learning things for our other classes. It would put a whole new meaning into our book reports!

We could also talk to other people on the Internet about what we are studying. This access would introduce us to new people and experiences we otherwise might never know. This communication is similar to writing a letter, but travels more quickly, and there is no cost for postage! People can now communicate with others around the world by typing messages on a computer.

To have access to the Internet on our own is very expensive. It requires a computer and an account to access the Internet. These accounts are arranged through services which can be very expensive. Since most of the colleges we students will be going on to will not only provide but also require computer usage, I think our school should do the same.

Thank you for your consideration.

NEW JERSEY

HSPA

High School Proficiency Assessment in

Language Arts

ANSWER SHEETS

HSPA – Practice Test 1
Answer Sheet

Writing: speculate

Reading: narrative

1.	Ⓐ	Ⓑ	Ⓒ	Ⓓ		6.	Ⓐ	Ⓑ	Ⓒ	Ⓓ
2.	Ⓐ	Ⓑ	Ⓒ	Ⓓ		7.	Ⓐ	Ⓑ	Ⓒ	Ⓓ
3.	Ⓐ	Ⓑ	Ⓒ	Ⓓ		8.	Ⓐ	Ⓑ	Ⓒ	Ⓓ
4.	Ⓐ	Ⓑ	Ⓒ	Ⓓ		9.	Ⓐ	Ⓑ	Ⓒ	Ⓓ
5.	Ⓐ	Ⓑ	Ⓒ	Ⓓ		10.	Ⓐ	Ⓑ	Ⓒ	Ⓓ

11.

12.

Writing: persuade

Reading: persuasive

1. Ⓐ Ⓑ Ⓒ Ⓓ   6. Ⓐ Ⓑ Ⓒ Ⓓ
2. Ⓐ Ⓑ Ⓒ Ⓓ   7. Ⓐ Ⓑ Ⓒ Ⓓ
3. Ⓐ Ⓑ Ⓒ Ⓓ   8. Ⓐ Ⓑ Ⓒ Ⓓ
4. Ⓐ Ⓑ Ⓒ Ⓓ   9. Ⓐ Ⓑ Ⓒ Ⓓ
5. Ⓐ Ⓑ Ⓒ Ⓓ   10. Ⓐ Ⓑ Ⓒ Ⓓ

11.

12.

Writing: revise/edit

HSPA – Practice Test 2
Answer Sheet

Writing: speculate

Reading: narrative

1. Ⓐ Ⓑ Ⓒ Ⓓ   6. Ⓐ Ⓑ Ⓒ Ⓓ
2. Ⓐ Ⓑ Ⓒ Ⓓ   7. Ⓐ Ⓑ Ⓒ Ⓓ
3. Ⓐ Ⓑ Ⓒ Ⓓ   8. Ⓐ Ⓑ Ⓒ Ⓓ
4. Ⓐ Ⓑ Ⓒ Ⓓ   9. Ⓐ Ⓑ Ⓒ Ⓓ
5. Ⓐ Ⓑ Ⓒ Ⓓ   10. Ⓐ Ⓑ Ⓒ Ⓓ

11.

12.

Writing: persuade

Reading: persuasive

1. Ⓐ Ⓑ Ⓒ Ⓓ
2. Ⓐ Ⓑ Ⓒ Ⓓ
3. Ⓐ Ⓑ Ⓒ Ⓓ
4. Ⓐ Ⓑ Ⓒ Ⓓ
5. Ⓐ Ⓑ Ⓒ Ⓓ

6. Ⓐ Ⓑ Ⓒ Ⓓ
7. Ⓐ Ⓑ Ⓒ Ⓓ
8. Ⓐ Ⓑ Ⓒ Ⓓ
9. Ⓐ Ⓑ Ⓒ Ⓓ
10. Ⓐ Ⓑ Ⓒ Ⓓ

11.

12.

Writing: revise/edit

NEW JERSEY

HSPA

High School Proficiency Assessment in

Language Arts

CLASS & HOMEWORK ASSIGNMENTS

Note: Answers and explanations to these Class & Homework Assignments are given in the Teacher's Guide, which is available from REA.

CLASS AND HOMEWORK ASSIGNMENTS

Language Arts

These assignments are provided with five answer choices each, as opposed to the HSPA's four answer choices. This results in a greater challenge and more rigorous preparation.

Reading Comprehension Questions

QUESTIONS 1–15 are based on the following passage. Read the passage carefully before choosing your answers.

From *Ethan Frome*
by Edith Wharton

It was there that, several years ago, I saw him for the first time; and the sight pulled me up sharp. Even then he was the most striking figure in Starkfield, though he was but the ruin of a man. It was not so much his great height that marked him, for the "natives" were easily singled out by their lank longitude from the stockier foreign breed: it was the careless powerful look he had, in spite of a lameness checking each step like the jerk of a chain. There was something bleak and unapproachable in his face, and he was so stiffened and grizzled that I took him for an old man and was surprised to hear that he was not more than fifty-two. I had this from Harmon Gow, who had driven the stage from Bettsbridge to Starkfield in pre-trolley days and knew the chronicle of all the families on his line.

Harmon drew a slab of tobacco from his pocket, cut off a wedge and pressed it into the leather pouch of his cheek. "Guess he's been in Starkfield too many winters. Most of the smart ones get away."

Though Harmon Gow developed the tale as far as his mental and moral reach permitted there were perceptible gaps between his facts, and I had the sense that the deeper meaning of the story was in the gaps. But one phrase stuck in my memory and served as the nucleus about which I grouped my subsequent inferences: "Guess he's been in Starkfield too many winters."

Before my own time there was up I had learned to know what that meant. Yet I had come in the degenerate day of trolley, bicycle and rural delivery, when communication was easy between the scattered mountain villages, and the bigger towns in the valleys, such as Bettsbridge and Shadd's Falls, had libraries, theatres and Y. M. C. A. halls to which the youth of the hills could descend for recreation. But when winter shut down on Starkfield, and the village lay under a sheet of snow perpetually renewed from the pale skies, I began to see what life there—or rather its negation—must have been in Ethan Frome's young manhood.

I had been sent up by my employers on a job connected with the big power-house at Corbury Junction, and a long-drawn carpenters' strike had so delayed the work that I found myself anchored at Starkfield—the nearest habitable spot—for the best part of the winter. I chafed at first, and then, under the hypnotising effect of routine, gradually began to find a grim satisfaction in the life. During the early part of my stay I had been struck by the contrast between the vitality of the climate and the deadness of the community. Day by day, after the December snows were over, a blazing blue sky poured down torrents of light and air on the white landscape, which gave them back in an intenser glitter. One would have supposed that such an atmosphere must quicken the emotions as well as the blood; but it seemed to produce no change except that of retarding still more the sluggish pulse of Starkfield. When I had been there a little longer, and had seen this phase of crystal clearness followed by long stretches of sunless cold; when the storms of February had pitched their white tents about the devoted village and the wild cavalry of March winds had charged down to their support, I began to understand why Starkfield emerged from its six months' siege like a starved garrison capitulating without quarter. Twenty years earlier the means of resistance must have been far fewer, and the enemy in command of almost all the lines of access between the beleaguered villages; and, considering these things, I felt the sinister force of Harmon's phrase: "Most of the smart ones get away." But if that were the case, how could any combination of obstacles have hindered the flight of a man like Ethan Frome?

1. **The phrase "checking each step like the jerk of a chain" is best interpreted to mean that Ethan**

    (A) had served time on a chain gang

    (B) moved about with uncertainty and timidity

(C) dragged along the dead weight of his injured leg

(D) was obviously one of the "stockier" breed

(E) bore the characteristics of a corrupt and criminal past

2. The phrase "singled out by their lank longitude" (lines 4–5) evokes the

(A) tall stature of the town "natives"

(B) sailing history of the townfolk

(C) prejudice "natives" had for their own kind

(D) animosity shown toward the "natives" by the foreigners in town

(E) "natives'" superiority over the foreign breed

3. The phrase "the storms of February pitched their white tents" presents an example of

(A) soliloquy   (D) ambiguity

(B) paradox   (E) dramatic irony

(C) personification

4. The narrator came to understand that life in the village was negated primarily because

(A) the townfolk were unsociable

(B) the long drawn carpenters' strike

(C) of the absence of the smart ones who got away

(D) of the degenerate influences of trolley, bicycle and rural delivery

(E) of the psychological isolation created by the weather

5. The image of a "starved garrison" is a reference to the

(A) beleaguered strikers

(B) shortage of food in the village

(C) militaristic nature of village life

(D) emotionally drained townfolk

(E) presence of government troops in the vicinity

6. In context, which of the following supports Harmon Gow's observation "Guess he's been in Starkfield too many winters"?

(A) Ethan's being the town's most striking figure

(B) Ethan's great height

(C) Ethan's careless, powerful look

(D) Ethan's bleak and unapproachable face

(E) Ethan's awareness of Gow's opinion of him

7. **In context, the phrase "degenerate day" is best interpreted to mean**

(A) a time when winters were more severe

(B) a time of inferior trolley and mail service

(C) an earlier time of restricted communication between villages

(D) the time when winter clamped down on the village

(E) a time of modern worldly influence on the village

8. **The final paragraph of the passage serves primarily to**

(A) relate how the narrator passed the winter

(B) illustrate Harmon Gow's comment about "too many winters"

(C) summarize the factors blocking Ethan's departure

(D) demonstrate the innate prejudice of Harmon Gow

(E) explain the folly of those who got away

9. **In the final paragraph, the narrator has difficulty**

(A) adjusting to the social life of the village

(B) understanding the villagers' joy at the approach of spring

(C) appreciating the beauty of the season

(D) comprehending the situation in the village in an earlier day

(E) reconciling the weather and its effect on the villagers

10. **In context, the "enemy" most likely represents**

(A) the degenerate influence of the world

(B) the hypnotizing effect of winter routine

(C) impassable snow and ice

(D) striking carpenters

(E) marauding cavalry

11. It can be inferred from the passage that

    (A) the narrator remained a stranger to the villagers

    (B) modern life had continued to pass the village by

    (C) the severe winters strengthened the bonds of the community

    (D) unusual circumstances compelled Ethan to stay there

    (E) Ethan enjoyed a warm relationship with the villagers

12. Which of the following best describes the narrator's view of the villagers at the end of the passage?

    (A) Closely knit community

    (B) A collection of weather beaten, phlegmatic individuals

    (C) A collection of inbred individuals who distrust strangers

    (D) Stout-hearted victors over nature

    (E) A collection of gossip mongers

13. The tone of the first paragraph is best described as

    (A) cynical glee.   (D) feigned sympathy.

    (B) sympathetic curiosity. (E) worshipful awe.

    (C) mild sarcasm.

14. In the lines "when the storms of February had pitched their white tents about the devoted village and the wild cavalry of March winds had charged down to their support," the narrator uses language that might best describe a

    (A) famine.   (D) medieval tournament.

    (B) Bedouin encampment.   (E) horse race.

    (C) hostile invasion.

15. All of the following represent figurative language EXCEPT

    (A) "the most striking figure in Starkfield"

    (B) "the leather pouch of his cheek"

    (C) "his mental and moral reach"

    (D) "I found myself anchored at Starkfield"

    (E) "pitched their white tents"

QUESTIONS 16-29 are based on the following passage. Read carefully before choosing your answers.

The Story of an Hour
by Kate Chopin

Knowing that Mrs. Mallard was afflicted with a heart trouble, great care was taken to break to her as gently as possible the news of her husband's death.

It was her sister Josephine who told her, in broken sentences, veiled hints that revealed in half concealing. Her husband's friend Richards was there, too, near her. It was he who had been in the newspaper office when intelligence of the railroad disaster was received, with Brently Mallard's name leading the list of "killed." He had only taken the time to assure himself of its truth by a second telegram, and had hastened to forestall any less careful, less tender friend in bearing the sad message.

She did not hear the story as many women have heard the same, with a paralyzed inability to accept its significance. She wept at once, with sudden, wild abandonment, in her sister's arms. When the storm of grief had spent itself she went away to her room alone. She would have no one follow her.

There stood, facing the open window, a comfortable, roomy arm-chair. Into this she sank, pressed down by a physical exhaustion that haunted her body and seemed to reach into her soul.

She could see in the open square before her house the tops of trees that were all aquiver with the new spring life. The delicious breath of rain was in the air. In the street below a peddler was crying his wares. The notes of a distant song which some one was singing reached her faintly, and countless sparrows were twittering in the eaves.

There were patches of blue sky showing here and there through the clouds that had met and piled above the other in the west facing her window.

She sat with her head thrown back upon the cushion of the chair quite motionless, except when a sob came up into her throat and shook her, as a child who has cried itself to sleep continues to sob in its dreams.

She was young, with a fair, calm face, whose lines bespoke repression and even a certain strength. But now there was a dull stare in her eyes, whose gaze was fixed away off yonder on one of those patches of blue sky. It was not a glance of reflection, but rather indicated a suspension of intelligent thought.

There was something coming to her and she was waiting for it, fearfully. What was it? She did not know; it was too subtle and elusive to name. But she felt it, creeping out of the sky, reaching toward her through the sound, the scents, the color that filled the air.

Now her bosom rose and fell tumultuously. She was beginning to recognize this thing that was approaching to possess her, and she was striving to beat it back with her will — as powerless as her two white slender hands would have been.

When she abandoned herself a little whispered word escaped her slightly parted lips. She said it over and over under her breath: "Free, free, free!" The vacant stare and the look of terror that had followed it went from her eyes. They stayed keen and bright. Her pulses beat fast, and the coursing blood warmed and relaxed every inch of her body.

She did not stop to ask if it were not a monstrous joy that held her. A clear and exalted perception enabled her to dismiss the suggestions as trivial.

She knew that she would weep again when she saw the kind, tender hands folded in death; the face that had never looked save with love upon her, fixed and gray and dead. But she saw beyond that bitter moment a long procession of years to come that would belong to her absolutely. And she opened and spread her arms out to them in welcome.

There would be no one to live for during those coming years; she would live for herself. There would be no powerful will bending her in that blind persistence with which men and women believe they have a right to impose a private will upon a fellow-creature. A kind intention or a cruel intention made the act seem no less a crime as she looked upon it in that brief moment of illumination.

And yet she had loved him — sometimes. Often she had not. What did it matter! What could love, the unsolved mystery, count for in face of this possession of self-assertion which she suddenly recognized for the strongest impulse of her being.

"Free! Body and soul free!" she kept whispering.

Josephine was kneeling before the closed door with her lips to the keyhole, imploring for admission. "Louise, open the door! I beg; open the door — you will make yourself ill. What are you doing, Louise? For heaven's sake open the door."

"Go away. I am not making myself ill." No; she was drinking in a very elixir of life through that open window.

Her fancy was running riot along those days ahead of her. Spring days, and summer days, and all sorts of days that would be her own. She breathed a quick prayer that life might be long. It was only yesterday she had thought with a shudder that life might be long.

She arose at length and opened the door to her sister's importunities. There was a feverish triumph in her eyes, and she carried herself unwittingly like a goddess of Victory. She clasped her sister's waist, and together they descended the stairs. Richards stood waiting for them at the bottom.

Some one was opening the front door with a latchkey. It was Brently Mallard who entered, a little travel-stained, composedly carrying his gripsack and umbrella. He had been far from the scene of accident, and did not even know there had been one. He stood amazed at Josephine's piercing cry; at Richards' quick motion to screen him from the view of his wife.

But Richards was too late.

When the doctors came they said she had died of heart disease — of joy that kills.

16. **Which of the first five sentences contains foreshadowing? Sentence number**

    (A) one   (D) four

    (B) two   (E) five

    (C) three

17. **All of the following are instances of irony EXCEPT**

    I.   the lines on Mrs. Mallard's face indicating repression

    II. Josephine's belief that Mrs. Mallard is making herself ill

    III. the doctor's belief that Mrs. Mallard died of joy at seeing her husband alive

    IV. Mrs. Mallard's anticipation of freedom and long life as she descends the stairs

    (A) I only   (D) II and III only

    (B) I and III only   (E) II and IV only

    (C) IV only

18. Mrs. Mallard's initial reaction to news of her husband's death can best be described as

   (A) hypocritical

   (B) sincere grief

   (C) uncomprehending

   (D) calculated to deceive others

   (E) puzzled

19. The details in the fifth paragraph suggest

   (A) sorrow

   (B) triviality

   (C) rebirth

   (D) death

   (E) alienation

20. Mrs. Mallard's joy at being free is first presented as something that she

   (A) has long desired

   (B) resists

   (C) believes is monstrous

   (D) is ashamed of

   (E) struggles to create

21. Mrs. Mallard's initial thoughts of freedom are depicted as

   (A) an external force that overpowers her

   (B) an immediate reaction to news of Brently Mallard's death

   (C) a manifestation of her self-centeredness

   (D) the result of a deliberate reasoning process

   (E) influenced by Josephine and Richards' presence

22. The kind of narration used in the story is

   (A) unreliable first-person

   (B) stream of consciousness

   (C) limited omniscience

   (D) objective

   (E) unreliable third-person

23. Which of the following LEAST accurately describes Brently Mallard?

   (A) Faithful

   (B) Abusive

   (C) Filled with good intentions

   (D) Loving

   (E) Tender

24. In her "brief moment of illumination," Mrs. Mallard's criticism is chiefly directed at

   (A) Brently Mallard.

   (B) the bonds of marriage.

   (C) herself.

   (D) society's expectations of widows.

   (E) her prior lack of educational opportunities.

25. In the line "as she looked upon it in that brief moment of illumination," "it" refers to

   (A) the conditions of life.

   (B) the sexual obligations of marriage.

   (C) lack of privacy in marriage.

   (D) unequal employment opportunities for women.

   (E) one person's will being dominated by another.

26. Mrs. Mallard thinks that it did not matter whether or not she had loved Brently Mallard because

   (A) death had separated them forever.

   (B) time will obliterate her memory of him.

   (C) her new sense of self makes her past life with him seem insignificant.

   (D) he had never made clear to her whether he loved her.

   (E) love is a mystery which can never be solved.

27. Mrs. Mallard's most important discovery is

   (A) that she is capable of living without Brently.

   (B) that she never loved Brently.

   (C) that people do not understand her.

   (D) her need for self-assertion.

   (E) her desire to escape from society.

28. The phrase "she carried herself unwittingly like a goddess of Victory" contains

    (A) personification.

    (B) a simile.

    (C) a paradox.

    (D) an apostrophe.

    (E) an invocation.

29. Which of the following statements about the last sentence of the story is LEAST accurate?

    (A) The author implies that Mrs. Mallard's death is just punishment for the "monstrous joy" she experienced earlier.

    (B) No character left alive at the end of the story fully understands Mrs. Mallard's death.

    (C) Mrs. Mallard has experienced great joy that intensifies her shock at seeing Brently alive.

    (D) The doctors are wrong in believing that Mrs. Mallard died of joy at seeing Brently alive.

    (E) The effectiveness of the last sentence depends on the reader understanding events more completely than the other characters who witness them.

QUESTIONS 30–45 are based on the following passage.

From "On Shakespeare and Milton"
by William Hazlitt

The great fault of a modern school of poetry is that it is an experiment to reduce poetry to a mere effusion of natural sensibility; or what is worse, to divest it both of imaginary splendor and human passion, to surround the meanest objects with the morbid feelings and devouring egotism of the writers' own minds. Milton and Shakespeare did not so understand poetry. They gave a more liberal interpretation both to nature and art. They did not do all they could to get rid of the one and the other, to fill up the dreary void with the Moods of their own Minds. They owe their power over the human mind to their having had a deeper sense than others of human life. But to the men I speak of there is nothing interesting, nothing heroical, but themselves. To them the fall of gods or of great men is the same. They do not enter into the feeling. They cannot understand the terms. They are even debarred from the last poor, paltry consolation of an unmanly triumph over fallen greatness; for their minds reject, with a convulsive effort and intolerable loathing, the very idea that there ever was, or was thought to be, anything superior to themselves. All that has ever excited the attention and admiration of the world, they look upon with the most perfect indifference; and they are surprised to find that the world repays their indifference with scorn. "With what measure they mete, it has been meted to them again."

Shakespeare's imagination is of the same plastic kind as his conception of character or passion. "It glances from heaven to earth." Its movement is rapid and devious. It unites the most opposite extremes: or, as Puck says, in boasting of his own feats, "puts a girdle round about the earth in forty minutes." He seems always hurrying from his subject, even while describing it; but the stroke, like the lightning's, is sure as it is sudden. He takes the widest possible range, but from that very range he has his choice of the greatest variety and aptitude of materials. He brings together images the most alike, but placed at the greatest distance from each other; that is, found in circumstances of the greatest dissimilitude. From the remoteness of his combinations, and the celerity with which they are effected, they coalesce the more indissolubly together.

30. **The primary distinction made in the first paragraph is one between**

    (A) the poetry of the senses and the poetry of imagination.

    (B) the modern school of poetry and that of Shakespeare and Milton.

    (C) the poetry of Shakespeare and the poetry of Milton.

    (D) the poetry of egotism and the poetry of sensibility.

    (E) the modern school of poetry and the poetry of human mood.

31. **Which of the following best describes the function of the first sentence in the first paragraph?**

    (A) It sarcastically provides evidence of the critic's intention.

    (B) It establishes the critic as an authority.

    (C) It clearly states the topic which the rest of the passage elucidates.

    (D) It directly addresses a common misconception to prepare the ground for a discussion of the critic's main topic.

    (E) It advances an accepted viewpoint that therefore does not need extensive support in the rest of the paragraph.

32. The critic cited here seems particularly upset by what he terms the modernist's

    (A) "moods."   (D) "human passion."

    (B) "morbid feelings."   (E) "intolerable loathing."

    (C) "egotism."

33. In context, the sentence "They gave a more liberal interpretation both to nature and art" suggests which of the following?

    (A) Shakespeare and Milton did not espouse the political conservatism of the modernists.

    (B) Shakespeare and Milton were tolerant in matters concerning nature and art.

    (C) Shakespeare and Milton did not understand poetry in the same way as the modernists.

    (D) The modernists had a greater right to their viewpoints than the Romantics.

    (E) The modern age is one of egotism.

34. The passage suggests that Classical Tragedy would not be of interest to the "modern school" because they

    (A) pay too much attention to their superiors and not enough to themselves.

    (B) do not see any difference between "the fall of gods or of great men."

    (C) they hate anything that holds the "admiration of the world."

    (D) they cannot deal with the scorn the critical world has for them.

    (E) they feel compelled to substitute their own "dreary world" for the real thing.

35. The author brings closure to his first paragraph by

    (A) stating that the modernists are as surprised at their reception as he is at their views.

    (B) implying that biblical injunctions are still in force, even though the modernists may be unbelievers.

(C) implying that the rest of the world is as indifferent to the modernists as they are to it.

(D) implying that the rest of the world scorns the modernists as much as he does.

(E) stating that there is nothing "heroical" in the modernist position.

36. **Stylistically, the second paragraph is best characterized by the repeated use of**

(A) descriptive adjectives. (D) assonance.

(B) action verbs. (E) alliteration.

(C) metaphor.

37. **The structure of the second paragraph is such that**

(A) most of the following sentences reinforce the contentions of the first sentence.

(B) the final sentence has been arrived at inductively.

(C) the central theme of the paragraph is stated in the middle of the paragraph.

(D) it relies heavily for contextual meaning on the statements of the first paragraph.

(E) each sentence is dependent on the previous one in establishing meaning.

38. **The critic demonstrates his admiration for Shakespeare in the second paragraph by**

(A) using images from literary critics to reinforce his argument.

(B) praising Shakespeare repeatedly for doing simple tasks well.

(C) using occasional quotes from Shakespeare's poetry.

(D) speaking of Shakespeare's works in the same manner as he speaks of Milton's.

(E) describing Shakespeare's importance in grandiose terms such as "celerity."

39. **The "girdle round about the earth" is best understood as**

(A) Shakespeare's universal appeal.

(B) Shakespeare's ability to give form to indiscriminate images.

(C) Shakespeare's ability to discuss all topics.

(D) Shakespeare's capacity to bring together extremes.

(E) Shakespeare's ability to communicate quickly using appropriate symbols.

40. The critic suggests light criticism of Shakespeare for his

(A) almost "plastic" conception of character.

(B) need to bring dissimilar images together.

(C) deviousness in character portrayal.

(D) hurrying from one subject to another.

(E) attempting to explain too much in his writing.

41. At the end of the second paragraph, the critic distinguishes between similar images and

(A) dissimilar meanings.   (D) indissoluble combinations.

(B) indissoluble materials.   (E) dissimilar circumstances.

(C) dissimilar ranges.

42. The critic focuses the reader's attention on Shakespeare by

(A) giving a plethora of examples from his works.

(B) the repeated use of pronouns for reference.

(C) making exaggerated claims as to the writer's genius.

(D) describing the Bard with Latin-based words of praise.

(E) attempting to describe Shakespeare's imagination.

43. The use of the words "dissimilitude" and "indissolubly" has the effect of

(A) providing closure with the opening contention in the first sentence of the second paragraph.

(B) providing poetic consonance that is appropriate to the discussion of Shakespeare's works.

(C) providing a point of contrast to concepts of similarity as advanced in the preceding sentences.

(D) providing parallelism between the ideas contained in the two sentences.

(E) providing a further description of the range of Shakespeare's writing.

44. **Hazlitt's two paragraphs might best be distinguished by which of the following stylistic changes?**

(A) A shortening of sentence length.

(B) Increased use of punctuation.

(C) Decreased attention to his opening contention.

(D) Increased attention to the foibles of the "modern school."

(E) Decreased use of descriptive adjectives.

45. **The development of the argument in paragraphs one and two can best be described as**

(A) moving from the specific to the general.

(B) moving from the speculative to the abstract.

(C) moving from the general to the specific.

(D) moving from the specific to the speculative.

(E) moving from contention to speculation.

QUESTIONS 46-54 are based on the following passage. Read the passage carefully and then answer the questions.

From "The Short, Happy Life of Francis Macomber"
by Ernest Hemingway

"I'd like to clear away the lion business," Macomber said. "It's not very pleasant to have your wife see you do something like that."

I should think it would be even more unpleasant to do it, Wilson thought, wife or no wife, or to talk about it having done it. But he said, "I wouldn't think about that any more. Any one could be upset by his first lion. That's all over."

But that night after dinner and a whisky and soda by the fire before going to bed, as Francis Macomber lay on his cot with the mosquito bar over him and listened to the night noises it was not all over. It was neither all over nor was it beginning. But more than shame he felt cold, hollow fear in him. The fear was still there like a cold slimy hollow in all the emptiness where once his confidence had been and it made him feel sick. It was still there with him now.

It had started the night before when he had wakened and heard the lion roaring somewhere up along the river. It was a deep sound and at the end there were sort of coughing grunts that made him seem just outside the tent, and when Francis Macomber woke in the night to hear it he was afraid. He could hear his wife breathing quietly, asleep. There was no one to tell he was afraid, nor to be afraid with him, and, lying alone, he did not know the Somali proverb that says a brave man is always frightened three times by a lion; when he first sees his track, when he first hears him roar and when he first confronts him. Then while they were eating breakfast by lantern light out in the dining tent, before the sun was up, the lion roared again and Francis thought he was just at the edge of camp.

"Sounds like an old-timer," Robert Wilson said, looking up from his kippers and coffee. "Listen to him cough."

"Is he very close?"

"A mile or so up the stream."

"Will we see him?"

"We'll have a look."

"Does his roaring carry that far? It sounds as though he were right in camp."

"Carries a hell of a long way," said Robert Wilson. "It's strange the way it carries. Hope he's a shootable cat. The boys said there was a very big one about here."

"If I get a shot, where should I hit him," Macomber asked, "to stop him?"

"In the shoulders," Wilson said. "In the neck if you can make it. Shoot for bone. Break him down."

"I hope I can place it properly," Macomber said.

"You shoot very well," Wilson told him. "Take your time. Make sure of him. The first one in is the one that counts."

46. Which of the following best indicates the subject of the passage?

   (A) Dealing with the apprehension of an impending confrontation.

   (B) Coping with life in the wild.

   (C) Dealing with a previous failure of courage.

   (D) Coping with marital difficulties.

   (E) Dealing with culture shock in a new situation.

47. Macomber's reflections reveal that the fledgling hunter is

   (A) uneasy about what his wife would think of his actions if she knew the truth.

   (B) angry at his wife for not having been with him when he needed her most.

   (C) afraid of his wife and what she will say about his cowardly actions.

   (D) embarrassed about his actions while his wife was looking on.

   (E) afraid that his cowardly actions in front of his wife have eroded his self-confidence.

48. The passage implies that Macomber first became fearful

   (A) when he confronted his first lion.

   (B) when he realized his wife was looking on as he confronted his first lion.

   (C) when he suspected that only he was afraid of the impending confrontation.

   (D) when he was eating breakfast just before the hunt.

   (E) only afterwards, when he fully realized the shame of what he had done.

49. The passage is most stylistically notable for

   (A) clear and precise descriptions of time placement.

   (B) clear and precise descriptions of fear.

   (C) clear and precise descriptions of geography and climate.

   (D) clear and precise descriptions of camp life.

   (E) clear and precise descriptions of the sounds of nature.

50. The chief effect of Hemingway's seemingly casual attention to punctuation and sentence length in this passage is to

    (A) contribute to a "stream of consciousness" atmosphere.

    (B) indicate that the personalities he is describing are marginally educated.

    (C) indicate that Macomber's emotional turmoil is great.

    (D) imply that these passages are not as important as those that will come later.

    (E) create a sense of detachment in the reader.

51. Which of the following best sums up the contrast between Macomber's attitude about his confrontation and that expressed by the Somali proverb?

    (A) Macomber is afraid, while the Somali proverb praises the "brave man."

    (B) Macomber is afraid, while the Somali proverb speaks of reasonable and prudent caution.

    (C) Macomber is really afraid of his wife's perceptions, not the lion.

    (D) Macomber thinks he is a coward, but the Somali proverb would indicate that he could still be a "brave man."

    (E) Macomber's cowardice renders him unable to appreciate the Somali wisdom.

52. Throughout the passage, Hemingway implies that the most important difference between Macomber and Wilson is that

    (A) Wilson is brave while Macomber is a coward.

    (B) Macomber is dependent on his wife, while Wilson lives independently.

    (C) Wilson is African while Macomber is an outsider.

    (D) Macomber is expressive, while Wilson is more restrained.

    (E) Wilson is experienced, while Macomber is inexperienced.

53. The nature of the dialogue between the men at the end of the passage is most indicative of

    (A) Macomber's limited attention and Wilson's complete absorption.

    (B) Macomber's curiosity and Wilson's casual interest.

(C) Macomber's fear and Wilson's bravery.

(D) Wilson's delight and Macomber's dread.

(E) Macomber's limited experience and Wilson's complete knowledge.

54. Macomber's comment that the lion's roar "sounds as though he were right in camp" implies that Macomber

(A) is woefully inexperienced in lion hunting.

(B) is not as yet sensitized to the atmospheric conditions of East Africa.

(C) is very apprehensive about the impending confrontation.

(D) has already determined that he will act in a cowardly manner.

(E) is not aware of the possibility that this lion is not "a shootable cat."

QUESTIONS 55–57 are based on the following passage.

From *Rascal*
by Sterling North

I had decided to let my raccoon make his own decision. But I took off his collar and his leash and put them in a pocket of my corduroy jacket as something to remember him by if he should choose to leave me. We sat together in the canoe, listening to the night sounds all around us, but for one sound in particular.

It came at last, the sound I had been waiting for, almost exactly like the crooning tremolo we had heard when the romantic female raccoon had tried to reach him through the chicken wire. Rascal became increasingly excited. Soon he answered with a slightly deeper crooning of his own. The female was now approaching along the edge of the stream, trilling a plaintive call, infinitely tender and questing. Rascal raced to the prow of the canoe, straining to see through the moonlight and shadow, sniffing the air, and asking questions.

"Do as you please, my little raccoon. It's your life," I told him.

He hesitated for a full minute, turned once to look back at me, then took the plunge and swam to the near shore. He had chosen to join that entrancing female somewhere in the shadows. I caught only one glimpse of them in a moonlit glade before they disappeared to begin their new life together.

55. **What is the overall tone of this passage?**

    (A) Uplifting   (D) Cynical

    (B) Melancholy   (E) Sarcastic

    (C) Forlorn

56. **Which of the following best describes the narrator's attitude toward his pet's departure?**

    (A) Sentimental   (D) Angry

    (B) Bitter yet resigned   (E) Tolerant but disappointed

    (C) Relieved

57. **The reader can infer that the narrator and his pet**

    (A) would soon forget about one another.

    (B) would never meet again.

    (C) were companions who understood each other.

    (D) would soon be united.

    (E) were never suited for one another.

    QUESTIONS 58–59 are based on the following passage.

From *A Tale of Two Cities*
by Charles Dickens

It was the best of times, it was the worst of times, it was the age of wisdom, it was the age of foolishness, it was the epoch of belief, it was the epoch of incredulity, it was the season of Light, it was the season of Darkness, it was the spring of hope, it was the winter of despair, we had everything before us, we had nothing before us, we were all going direct to Heaven, we were all going direct the other way—in short, the period was so far like the present period, that some of its noisiest authorities insisted on its being received, for good or for evil, in the superlative degree of comparison only.

There were a king with a large jaw, and a queen with a plain face, on the throne of England; there were a king with a large jaw, and a queen with a fair face, on the throne of France. In both countries it was clearer than crystal to the lords of the State preserves of loaves and fishes, that things in general were settled for ever.

58. The vast comparisons in the above passage indicate that the speaker is describing

    (A) a placid historical time period.

    (B) a time of extreme political upheaval.

    (C) a public event.

    (D) a time when anything was possible.

    (E) a time in the distant past.

59. The last sentence of the passage

    (A) mocks the self-assuredness of the governments of England and France.

    (B) comments on the horrible poverty of the two nations.

    (C) most likely foreshadows an upcoming famine or drought.

    (D) attacks the two governments for neglecting the poor, hungry masses.

    (E) celebrates the wisdom of the lords of state.

QUESTIONS 60 to 62 refer to the following excerpt.

From *All the Sad Young Men*
by F. Scott Fitzgerald

"About Judy Jones."

Devlin looked at him helplessly.

"Well, that's—I told you all there is to it. He treats her like the devil. Oh, they're not going to get divorced or anything. When he's particularly outrageous she forgives him. In fact, I'm inclined to think she loves him. She was a pretty girl when she first came to Detroit."

A pretty girl! The phrase struck Dexter as ludicrous. "Isn't she a pretty girl, any more?"

"Oh, she's all right."

"Look here," said Dexter, sitting down suddenly. "I don't understand. You say she was a 'pretty girl' and now she's 'all right.' I don't understand what you mean—Judy Jones wasn't a pretty girl, at all. She was a great beauty. Why, I knew her. I knew her. She was—"

Devlin laughed pleasantly.

"I'm not trying to start a row," he said. "I think Judy's a nice girl and I like her. I can't understand how a man like Lud Simms could fall madly in love with her, but he did." Then he added: "Most of the women like her."

Dexter looked closely at Devlin, thinking wildly that there must be a reason for this, some insensitivity in the man or some private malice.

"Lots of women fade just like that," Devlin snapped his fingers. "You must have seen it happen. Perhaps I've forgotten how pretty she was at her wedding. I've seen her so much since then, you see. She has nice eyes."

A sort of dullness settled down upon Dexter. For the first time in his life he felt like getting very drunk. He knew that he was laughing loudly at something Devlin had said, but he did not know what it was or why it was funny. When, in a few minutes, Devlin went he lay down on his lounge and looked out the window at the New York skyline into which the sun was sinking in dull lovely shades of pink and gold.

He had thought that having nothing else to lose he was invulnerable at last—but he knew that he had just lost something more, as surely as if he had married Judy Jones and seen her fade before his eyes.

60. **The underlying meaning of the last paragraph is**

    (A) Dexter is saddened but relieved that he never married Judy.

    (B) Judy was never meant for Dexter.

    (C) even though they never married, Dexter is still touched by Judy's life.

    (D) nothing can hurt Dexter any more than Judy did.

    (E) he still wishes that he and Judy could be united.

61. **Which of the following quotations does not apply to Dexter's situation concerning Judy?**

    (A) It is impossible to love and be wise. —Francis Bacon, *Of Love*

    (B) Love is blind. —Geoffrey Chaucer, "The Merchant," from *The Canterbury Tales*

    (C) Love comforteth like sunshine after rain. —Shakespeare, *Venus and Adonis*

(D) Speak of me as I am, one that loved not wisely but too well.
—Shakespeare, *Othello*

(E) Love blinds all men alike, both the reasonable, and the foolish.
—Meander, *Andria*

62. **From this dialogue, we can conclude that Devlin is being**

(A) argumentative and harsh.

(B) realistic but kind.

(C) pessimistic and unforgiving.

(D) optimistic and charitable.

(E) rude but accurate.

QUESTIONS 63 to 69 refer to the following essay.

"A Balm for Fishlessness"
by Arnold Gingrich

In a sense I never fish alone, in that a good share of the time, even before dawn and after dark, I'm apt to be fishing "with somebody." It may be somebody I've never known nor ever will, or it may be somebody I have known but will never see again. Because it's with somebody who is in any case absent from the actual scene of my fishing, my own more-than-middle age and the law of averages team up to furnish the likelihood that it is somebody who is no longer living. But that's only natural in any event; you can learn more from the dead than from the living, if only because there are so many more of them. But I still don't mean that all my fishing is "down among the dead men." I'm as ready as the next to take a tip from any passing stranger, when I'm somewhere out on a stream.

Of course, the more you fish, the sooner you reach that stage where you'd rather put the fish back for somebody else to catch, or simply to catch them again yourself rather than take them home to eat, or even to have mounted, for the subsequent amazement of all and sundry.

You'd think, then, that as long as we're not going to keep the fish anyway, going fishless wouldn't be such a dire fate as to warrant our being classified as hardship cases. What's so bad about being skunked, if you set out resolved to return as empty-handed as if you had been anyway? And why moan about the one that got away, when you were going to put him back again even if he hadn't? Well, this is where the element of thinking about it enters in. It only matters, of course, if you think it does. And boy, you find it very hard to think of anything, at least at that moment, that matters more. In fact, the great thing about fishing is that there are very few activities that are open to all men on a virtually equal basis and that can provide you with occasions to feel quite so deeply, to care quite that much.

It's all very well for Izzak Walton to have settled the question centuries ago, on a purely philosophical basis, by reminding us that no man can be said to have lost that which he never had. On that basis, of course, there is no such thing as a lost fish. But if it doesn't exist, why does it hurt so much?

I've never felt such intense compassion for anyone in my life as I felt for Ernest Hemingway in Bimini in 1936, when a marlin that looked the size of a tank car in the sun got away after some thirty jumps, and the hand-forged hook, looking the size of an anchor, came back, pulled out and straightened like a bent bobby-pin. And if I felt that bad, then how bad did he feel?

63. **Concerning Izzak Walton's philosophy and fish which get away, the speaker**

   (A) totally agrees with Izzak Walton.

   (B) does not understand Walton's philosophy.

   (C) applies Walton's wisdom to his own experience.

   (D) totally disagrees with Walton's premise.

   (E) needs to learn more about the matter.

64. **The speaker believes that if a person cannot lose that which he/she never had, then**

   (A) you can never gain something you never had.

   (B) something which you nearly had is never really lost.

   (C) material objects are never really lost.

   (D) anything immaterial can never be lost.

   (E) you also can never really win anything.

65. **In the final paragraph, the fisherman suggests that Ernest Hemingway's feelings about his lost marlin in Bimini were probably**

(A) stronger than his own emotions.

(B) hidden.

(C) the same as Izzak Walton's philosophy.

(D) known to the public.

(E) not as strong as his own feelings.

66. **You can conclude from the passage that if the act of fishing is a balm to the fisherman, then**

(A) no one actually needs to catch fish.

(B) more fishermen would have healthier personalities.

(C) going fishless could still be rewarding.

(D) other sports can be just as therapeutic.

(E) doctors would not be needed.

67. **Referring to the third paragraph, if you "got skunked," you would**

(A) not have made a big catch.

(B) have made your fishing limit.

(C) come home empty-handed.

(D) be disappointed.

(E) encounter a foul-smelling animal.

68. **In the first paragraph, the fisherman says that he is never alone because**

(A) thoughts and memories of people, both known and unknown, are always with him.

(B) visions of his dead friends come back to him.

(C) interesting strangers always stop by.

(D) he does not actually need company.

(E) fishing is a solitary venture.

69. The speaker's assumptions about his future fishing companions imply that the fisherman will probably fish once again with friends, dead or still alive, because

(A) he believes in reincarnation.

(B) this sport is probably not confined to people only on this earth.

(C) he happens to be joking.

(D) he is only fantasizing.

(E) None of the above.

QUESTIONS 70-75 refer to the following excerpt .

From *The Apprenticeship of Duddy Kravitz*
by Mordecai Richler

The man to avoid, as far as strappings went, was Mr Coldwell. Mr Coldwell strapped from an angle, so that the tongue curled around your hand and rebounded hard on the wrist. Usually he strapped a boy until he cried; then he'd say, "I'd hoped you'd take it like a man." Next came Mr. Feeney. Mr Feeney took three steps backwards with the strap resting lightly on his shoulder, charged, and struck. Mr MacPherson, however, did not even know how to hold the strap properly. So when he led Duddy Kravitz into the Medical Room that afternoon, breaking with a practice of twenty years, the actual blows were feeble, and it was Duddy who emerged triumphant, racing outside to greet his classmates.

"Hey, look! Look, jerkos! Ten on each. Mac strapped me. Mac, of all people."

Mr MacPherson strapped fifteen boys that week, and his method improved with practice. But the rowdiness in class, and his own drinking, increased in proportion to the strappings. He began to sit around the house alone. He seldom went out any more.

And then one night, a couple of weeks after he had returned to school, Mr MacPherson sat down before his dead fireplace and broke open a new bottle of whiskey. He sat there for hours, cherishing old and unlikely memories and trying to feel something more than a sense of liberation because Jenny, whom he had once loved truly, was dead. Half the bottle was finished before all of Mr MacPherson's troubles crystallized into the hard, leering shape of Duddy Kravitz. Mr MacPherson chuckled. Staggering into the hall, pulling the light cord so hard that it broke off in his hand, he rocked to and fro over the telephone. It did not take him long, considering his state, to find Kravitz's number, and he dialed it with care. The telephone must have rung and rung about fifteen times before somebody answered it.

"Hello," a voice said gruffly.

Mr MacPherson didn't reply.

"*Hullo.* H U L L O! Who is that anyway? Hullo."

It wasn't Kravitz. He would have recognized Kravitz's voice. The room began to sway around Mr MacPherson.

"Who's speaking?" the voice commanded.

"Mr MacPhers—"

Mr MacPherson slammed the receiver back on the hook and stumbled into the living-room, knocking over a lamp on his way. The first thing he saw there were the history test papers. He ripped them apart, flung them into the fireplace, and lit them. Exhausted, he collapsed into his armchair to watch them burn.

70. **From the first few lines, you can tell that Mr. Coldwell**

    (A) believes discipline builds character.

    (B) is a very knowledgeable man.

    (C) has been a teacher for a long time.

    (D) does not enjoy punishing students.

    (E) enjoys teaching school.

71. **When Duddy Kravitz gets the strap, he is**

    (A) sorrowful.   (D) boastful.

    (B) angry.   (E) indifferent.

    (C) disappointed.

72. **From the description of Mr. MacPherson as he breaks open a new whiskey bottle, we can infer that he**

    (A) has an unhappy marriage.

(B)   suffers from increasing frustration.

(C)   wants to move to another city.

(D)   is a skilled teacher and disciplinarian.

(E)   drinks because he enjoys being drunk.

73. **From a close reading of Mr. MacPherson's thoughts of Duddy, we can form this analogy: Mr. MacPherson's thoughts about Duddy Kravitz are like**

(A)   water on a fire.

(B)   a cold drink on a hot day.

(C)   grains of sand in an oyster.

(D)   money in a rich man's wallet.

(E)   food to a hungry person.

74. **Judging by Mr. MacPherson's attempt to telephone Duddy Kravitz, we can conclude that he wanted to**

(A)   congratulate Duddy.

(B)   speak to Duddy's parents.

(C)   get Duddy to come over for an honest talk.

(D)   tell Duddy what he really thought of him.

(E)   have Duddy help him mark the history papers.

75. **The burning of the papers most nearly means that Mr. MacPherson**

(A)   was expressing his hatred of his life.

(B)   was at last happy.

(C)   will make a new start in life.

(D)   would no longer teach history.

(E)   would finally get over Jenny's death.

QUESTIONS 76-83 refer to the following conversation.

From *Of Mice and Men*
by John Steinbeck

George still stared morosely at the fire. "When I think of the swell time I could have without you, I go nuts. I never get no peace."

Lennie still knelt. He looked off into the darkness across the river. "George, you want I should go away and leave you alone?"

"Where the hell could you go?"

"Well, I could go off in the hills there. Some place I'd find a cave."

"Yeah? How'd you eat? You ain't got sense enough to find nothing to eat."

"I'd find things, George. I don't need no nice food with ketchup. I'd lay out in the sun and nobody'd hurt me. An' if I foun' a mouse, I could keep it. Nobody'd take it away from me."

George looked quickly and searchingly at him. "I been mean, ain't I?"

"If you don' want me I can go off in the hills and find a cave. I can go away any time."

"No—look! I was jus' foolin', Lennie. 'Cause I want you to stay with me. Trouble with mice is you always kill 'em." He paused. "Tell you what I'll do, Lennie. First chance I get I'll give you a pup. Maybe you wouldn't kill it. That'd be better than mice. And you could pet it harder."

Lennie avoided the bait. He had sensed his advantage. "If you don't want me, you only jus' got to say so, and I'll go off in those hills right there—right up in those hills and live by myself. An' I won't get no mice stole from me."

George said, "I want you to stay with me, Lennie, Jesus Christ, somebody'd shoot you for a coyote if you was by yourself. No, you stay with me. Your Aunt Clara wouldn't like you running off by yourself, even if she is dead."

Lennie spoke craftily, "Tell me—like you done before."

"Tell you what?"

"About the rabbits."

George snapped, "You ain't gonna put nothing over on me."

Lennie pleaded, "Come on, George. Tell me, please George. Like you done before."

"You get a kick outta that, don't you? Awright, I'll tell you, and then we'll eat our supper...." George's voice became deeper. He repeated his words rhythmically as though he had said them many times before....

Lennie was delighted. "That's it—that's it. Now tell how it is with us."

George went on. "With us it ain't like that. We got a future. We got somebody to talk to that gives a damn about us. We don't have to sit in no barroom blowin' our jack jus because we got no place to go...."

"O.K. Someday—we're gonna get the jack together and we're gonna have a little house and a couple of acres an' a cow and some pigs and—"

"An' live off the fatta the lan'!," Lennie shouted.

76. **You can tell from the dialogue that**

    (A) each man is bonded in friendship with the other.

    (B) neither one really cares what happens to the other.

    (C) George will stay angry with Lennie this time.

    (D) Lennie sincerely intends to leave.

    (E) George intends to abandon Lennie soon.

77. **It becomes clear when studying the conversation that**

    (A) George has little compassion for Lennie.

    (B) Lennie has learned to manipulate George.

    (C) George has the "upper hand" at all times.

    (D) Lennie intends to hurt George.

    (E) Lennie is a survivor.

78. **You can best compare the relationship of George and Lennie with one of**

(A) best friends.   (D) feuding neighbors.

(B) father and son.   (E) complete strangers.

(C) casual acquaintances.

79. **George's transition between fantasizing about life without Lennie and appeasing him provide insight into**

(A) George's inner conflict.

(B) George's intelligence.

(C) Lennie's attitude.

(D) both men's devotion to each other.

(E) George's impatience.

80. **The fact that Lennie accidentally kills mice while he pets them indicates**

(A) he is careless.   (D) he is kind.

(B) he is cruel.   (E) he is stubborn.

(C) he is not aware of his own strength.

81. **The conflict within George appears to be one concerning**

(A) his relationship with Lennie.

(B) his lack of money.

(C) his lack of education.

(D) his job.

(E) his bad luck.

82. **The fact that Lennie knows George's story by heart means**

(A) Lennie created it.

(B) he has heard it many times.

(C) it is probably untrue.

(D) there is cause for concern.

(E) nothing in particular.

83. **Essentially the story gives each man**

 (A) something to talk about.   (D) cause for concern.

 (B) hope for the future.   (E) nothing in particular.

 (C) reason to leave town.

QUESTIONS 84 to 88 refer to the following passage.

From "The Legend of Sleepy Hollow"
by Washington Irving

The schoolmaster is generally a man of some importance in the female circle of a rural neighborhood; being considered a kind of idle gentlemanlike personage, of vastly superior taste and accomplishments to the rough country swains, and, indeed, inferior in learning only to the parson. His appearance, therefore, is apt to occasion some little stir at the tea-table of a farmhouse, and the addition of a supernumerary dish of cakes or sweetmeats, or, peradventure, the parade of a silver tea-pot. Our man of letters, therefore, was peculiarly happy in the smiles of all the country damsels. How he would figure among them in the churchyard, between services on Sundays! Gathering grapes for them from the wild vines that overrun the surrounding trees; reciting for their amusement all the epitaphs on the tombstones; or sauntering, with a whole bevy of them, along the banks of the adjacent mill-pond; while the more bashful country bumpkins hung sheepishly back, envying his superior elegance and address.

From his half itinerant life, also, he was a kind of travelling gazette, carrying the whole budget of local gossip from house to house; so that his appearance was always greeted with satisfaction. He was, moreover, esteemed by the women as a man of great erudition, for he had read several books quite through, and was a perfect master of Cotton Mather's History of New England Witchcraft, in which, by the way, he most firmly and potently believed.

84. **The first two sentences suggest that the local schoolmaster**

 (A) is highly esteemed by all.

 (B) is held in high esteem particularly by the women.

 (C) is not held in high regard.

 (D) is considered a "country bumpkin."

 (E) is held in higher esteem than the parson.

85. **From sentences 3–5, the reader can infer that the schoolmaster**

    (A) is clearly shy and retiring.

    (B) is modest and unassuming.

    (C) is extremely humble.

    (D) thrives on all this attention.

    (E) strives to keep out of the limelight.

86. **In context, "half itinerant" means**

    (A) he wandered through the countryside a great deal.

    (B) he was only half literate.

    (C) his life was only half fulfilled.

    (D) he had two jobs.

    (E) None of the above.

87. **The lines describing his "half-itinerant life" suggest that the schoolmaster**

    (A) sold newspapers.

    (B) engaged in gossiping with the ladies.

    (C) was a man of high esteem.

    (D) never encouraged gossiping.

    (E) was on a very strict budget.

88. **The final sentence leads the reader to conclude that the school-master**

    (A) was well read.

    (B) was well educated.

    (C) was well read in certain subjects.

    (D) loved classical literature.

    (E) enjoyed reading fiction.

    QUESTIONS 89–99 are based on the following passage.

From "The Horse Dealer's Daughter"
by D.H. Lawrence

She had suffered badly during the period of poverty. Nothing, however, could shake the curious, sullen, animal pride that dominated each member of the family. Now, for Mabel, the end had come. Still she would not cast about her. She would follow her own way just the same. She would always hold the keys of her own situation. Mindless and persistent, she endured from day to day. Why should she think? Why should she answer anybody? It was enough that this was the end, and there was no way out. She need not pass any more darkly along the main street of the small town, avoiding every eye. She need not demean herself any more, going into the shops and buying the cheapest food. This was at an end. She thought of nobody, not even of herself. Mindless and persistent, she seemed in a sort of ecstasy to be coming nearer to her fulfillment, her own glorification, approaching her dead mother, who was glorified.

In the afternoon, she took a little bag, with shears and sponge and a small scrubbing-brush, and went out. It was a gray, wintry day, with saddened dark green fields and an atmosphere blackened by the smoke of foundries not far off. She went quickly, darkly along the causeway, heeding nobody, through the town to the churchyard.

There she always felt secure, as if no one could see her, although as a matter of fact she was exposed to the stare of everyone who passed along under the churchyard wall. Nevertheless, once under the shadow of the great looming church, among the graves, she felt immune to the world, reserved within the thick churchyard wall as in another country.

Carefully, she clipped the grass from the grave, and arranged the pinky-white, small chrysanthemums in the tin cross. When this was done, she took an empty jar from a neighboring grave, brought water, and carefully, most scrupulously sponged the marble headstone and coping-stone.

It gave her sincere satisfaction to do this. She felt in immediate contact with the world of her mother. She took minute pains, went through the park in a state bordering on pure happiness, as if in performing this task she came into a subtle, intimate connection with her mother. For the life she followed here in the world was far less real than the world of death she inherited from her mother.

89. **Which of the following best summarizes the subject of the first paragraph of the passage?**

   (A) The debilitating effect of poverty on a family

   (B) The liberating effects of impoverishment

   (C) The ability of hope to overcome the debilitating effects of poverty

(D) The ecstasy that results when death is imminent

(E) The insanity caused by total despair

90. **The tone of the author towards Mabel is**

    (A) sympathetic.

    (B) sarcastic.

    (C) horrified.

    (D) patronizing.

    (E) uninterested.

91. **The author implies that Mabel's questioning**

    (A) is an act of information gathering.

    (B) is an expression of self-doubt.

    (C) is a defiant expression of self-assurance.

    (D) is simply an attempt by the author to indicate what she is thinking.

    (E) is an attempt by the author to gain the reader's sympathy for her situation.

92. **The attainment of glory is associated in Mabel's mind with**

    (A) the attainment of riches.

    (B) the loss of riches.

    (C) the pursuit of spiritual immortality.

    (D) the arrival of death.

    (E) the triumph of the individual mind.

93. **Mabel's liberation from misery is based mostly on the fact that she**

    (A) no longer has to contend with poverty.

    (B) is full of a sullen pride, like the rest of her family.

    (C) no longer thinks of herself.

    (D) has grown closer to her dead mother.

    (E) no longer has to demean herself when she goes to town.

94. **The second paragraph of this selection is remarkable stylistically in that it**

(A) portrays a woman more involved with death than with life.

(B) sustains a pattern of death imagery almost throughout.

(C) concentrates on seemingly unimportant minor details.

(D) uses natural description to portray Mabel's despair.

(E) is written in a style unlike the surrounding paragraphs.

95. **The author's placement of the description of Mabel's bag in the same paragraph with the description of the landscape**

(A) underscores the stylistic challenges the author typically presents to the reader.

(B) indicates that Mabel is as intent on eliminating the grime of her life as she is in "scrubbing" the soot off her mother's grave.

(C) foreshadows her impending suicide.

(D) is meant to indicate the disorder of her mind; no well-adjusted person would go out in this weather.

(E) reinforces the picture of Mabel as a character who gives no outward indication of her "dark" intentions.

96. **The third paragraph of this passage ("There she always...") presents the reader with the basic contradiction that**

(A) Mabel believes the graveyard will not hide her; she is more obvious to the prying public when she goes there.

(B) Mabel feels immune from the world even though she is more exposed to it.

(C) Mabel can feel most alive surrounded by a world of death.

(D) Mabel can only find independence by communing with the spirit of her dead mother.

(E) Mabel can only feel secure within the insecure and threatening world of death.

97. **The details supplied in the description of the graveyard clearing indicate that**

(A) Mabel has not cleaned the grave in a long time.

(B) Mabel is unique in cleaning her mother's grave.

(C) cleaning her mother's grave is a fulfilling, even happy task.

(D) it is unusual for Mabel to clean the grave alone.

(E) headstone cleaning is a seasonal occurrence.

98. **Mabel enjoys cleaning her mother's grave because**

    (A) she believes she is defying the world of death by entering its confines.

    (B) she is able to escape her real world of troubles by contemplating the afterlife.

    (C) she feels she is returning all the favors her mother did for her when she was alive

    (D) she enjoys the park-like atmosphere of the graveyard.

    (E) she comes in contact with the more real world of death.

99. **The churchyard wall represents for Mabel**

    (A) the boundary between the living and the dead.

    (B) a border between her native land and that of foreigners.

    (C) a mere physical obstacle of little consequence.

    (D) a forbidding symbol of death.

    (E) a religious boundary, representing hallowed ground.

Essay Questions from Prompts

Essay 1

DIRECTIONS: You will have 45 minutes to plan and write an essay on the topic specified. Read the topic carefully. Do not write on a topic other than the one specified. An essay on a topic of your own choice is not acceptable. Remember that how well you write is much more important than how much you write.

Essay Topic

The old saying, "experience is the best teacher," suggests to some people that they would benefit more from learning on the job or in the world than from continuing their formal education in the school or college classroom.

Assignment: Write an essay in which you discuss the relative values of experiential and academic learning. Support your view with specific examples from literature, history, current events, or personal experience.

Essay 2

DIRECTIONS: You will have 45 minutes to plan and write an essay on the topic specified. Read the topic carefully. Do not write on a topic other than the one specified. An essay on a topic of your own choice is not acceptable. Remember that how well you write is much more important than how much you write.

Essay Topic

Young people seem very conscious of wearing "trendy" or "brand name" clothing, especially the kind endorsed by sports figures or associated with popular musicians.

Assignment: Does this behavior reinforce or argue against the idea that "clothes make the man [or woman]"? Support your answer with specific examples.

Essay 3

DIRECTIONS: You will have 60 minutes to plan and write an essay on the topic specified. Read the topic carefully. Do not write on a topic other than the one specified. An essay on a topic of your own choice is not acceptable. Remember that how well you write is much more important than how much you write.

Essay Topic

Some misconceptions seem so accepted by the general public that they lead to derogatory stereotypes.

Assignment: Write an essay in which you assume a position about the topic and support it. Use appropriate and effective language and make sure to develop ideas logically.

Essay Questions From Passages

QUESTION 1. *(Suggested time — 40 minutes.)* In the selection below, Joseph Conrad describes a boat trip up the Congo River and the psychological and physical effects that trip has on the narrator. Read the passage carefully. Then write an essay in which you describe the psychological stresses and the physical demands that the narrator endured. Use specific references to the text to show how Conrad's diction, syntax, and use of detail served to convey those demands.

From "Heart of Darkness"
by Joseph Conrad

Going up the river was like travelling back to the earliest beginnings of the world, when vegetation rioted on the earth and the big trees were kings. An empty stream, a great silence, an impenetrable forest. The air was warm, thick, heavy, sluggish. There was no joy in the brilliance of sunshine. The long stretches of the waterway ran on, deserted, into the gloom of overshadowed distances. On silvery sandbanks hippos and alligators sunned themselves side by side. The broadening waters flowed through a mob of wooded islands; you lost your way on that river as you would in a desert, and butted all day long against shoals, trying to find the channel, till you thought yourself bewitched and cut off forever from everything you had known once — somewhere — far away — in another existence perhaps. There were moments when one's past came back to one, as it will sometimes when you have not a moment to spare to yourself; but it came in the shape of an unrestful and noisy dream, remembered with wonder amongst the overwhelming realities of this strange world of plants, and water, and silence. And this stillness of life did not in the least resemble a peace. It was the stillness of an implacable force brooding over an inscrutable intention. It looked at you with a vengeful aspect. I got used to it afterwards; I did not see it any more; I had no time. I had to keep guessing at the channel; I had to discern, mostly by inspiration, the signs of hidden banks; I watched for sunken stones; I was learning to clap my teeth smartly before my heart flew out, when I shaved by a fluke some infernal sly old snag that would have ripped the life out of the tin-pot steamboat and drowned all the pilgrims; I had to keep a look-out for the signs of dead wood we could cut up in the night for next day's steaming. When you have to attend to things of that sort, to the mere incidents of the surface, the reality — the reality, I tell you — fades. The inner truth is hidden — luckily, luckily. But I felt it all the same; I felt often its mysterious stillness watching me at my monkey tricks....

QUESTION 2. *(Suggested time — 40 minutes.)* Read the passage below carefully. Then write an essay explaining the narrator's attitude toward the "speaker" and analyzing the techniques the narrator uses to define the "speaker's" character.

From *Hard Times*
by Charles Dickens

"Now, what I want is Facts. Teach these boys and girls nothing but Facts. Facts alone are wanted in life. Plant nothing else, and root out everything else. You can only form the minds of reasoning animals upon Facts: nothing else will ever be of any service to them. This is the principle on which I bring up my own children, and this is the principle on which I bring up these children. Stick to Facts, sir!"

The scene was a plain, bare, monotonous vault of a school-room, and the speaker's square forefinger emphasized his observations by underscoring every sentence with a line on the schoolmaster's sleeve. The emphasis was helped by the speaker's square wall of a forehead, which had his eyebrows for its base, while his eyes found commodious cellarage in two dark caves, overshadowed by the wall. The emphasis was helped by the speaker's voice, which was inflexible, dry, and dictatorial. The emphasis was helped by the speaker's hair, which bristled on the skirts of his bald head, a plantation of firs to keep the wind from its shining surface, all covered with knobs, like the crust of a plum pie, as if the head had scarcely warehouse-room for the hard facts stored inside. The speaker's obstinate carriage, square coat, square legs, square shoulders—nay, his very neckcloth, trained to take him by the throat with an unaccommodating grasp, like a stubborn fact, as it was—all helped the emphasis.

"In this life, we want nothing but Facts, sir; nothing but Facts!"

The speaker, and the schoolmaster, and the third grown person present, all backed a little, and swept with their eyes the inclined plane of little vessels then and there arranged in order, ready to have imperial gallons of facts poured into them until they were full to the brim.

QUESTION 3. *(Suggested time — 40 minutes.)* The passage below is the opening of a short story. Read the passage carefully. Then write an essay in which you define the stylistic techniques by which the author attempts to create an atmosphere of horror. Refer to the text of the passage wherever appropriate.

From "The Fall of The House of Usher"
by Edgar Allan Poe

During the whole of a dull, dark, and soundless day in the autumn of the year, when the clouds hung oppressively low in the heavens, I had been passing alone, on horseback, through a singularly dreary tract of country, and at length found myself, as the shades of the evening drew on, within view of the melancholy House of Usher. I know not how it was — but, with the first glimpse of the building, a sense of insufferable gloom pervaded my spirit. I say insufferable; for the feeling was unrelieved by any of that half-pleasurable, because poetic, sentiment with which the mind usually receives even the sternest natural images of the desolate or terrible. I looked upon the scene before me — upon the mere house, and the simple landscape features of the domain — upon the bleak walls — upon the vacant eye-like windows — upon a few rank sedges — and upon a few white trunks of decayed trees — with an utter depression of soul which I can compare to no earthly sensation more properly to the after-dream of the reveller upon opium — the bitter lapse into every-day life — the hideous dropping off of the veil. There was an iciness, a sinking, a sickening of the heart — an unredeemed dreariness of thought which no goading of the imagination could torture into aught of the sublime. What was it — I paused to think — what was it that unnerved me in the contemplation of the House of Usher?

QUESTION 4. *(Suggested time — 35 minutes.)* The passage quoted below is the opening of Thoreau's persuasive essay "Civil Disobedience." Read the passage carefully. Then write an essay in which you analyze the strategies or devices (organization, diction, tone, use of detail) that make Thoreau's appeal compelling and effective for his educated audience.

From *"Civil Disobedience"*
by Henry David Thoreau

I heartily accept the motto, — "That government is best which governs least"; and I should like to see it acted up to more rapidly and systematically. Carried out, it finally amounts to this, which also I believe, — "That government is best which governs not at all"; and when men are prepared for it, that will be the kind of government which they will have. Government is at best but an expedient; but most governments are usually, and all governments are sometimes, inexpedient. The objections which have been brought against a standing army, and they are many and weighty, and deserve to prevail, may also at last be brought against a standing government. The government itself, which is only the mode which the people have chosen to execute their will, is equally liable to be abused and perverted before the people can act through it. Witness the present Mexican war, the work of comparatively a few individuals using the standing government as their tool; for, in the outset, the people would not have consented to this measure.

This American government — what is it but a tradition, though a recent one, endeavoring to transmit itself unimpaired to posterity, but each instant losing some of its integrity? It has not the vitality and force of a single living man; for a single man can bend it to his will. It is a sort of wooden gun to the people themselves. But it is not the less necessary for this; for the people must have that idea of government which they have. Governments show thus how successfully men can be imposed on, even impose on themselves, for their own advantage. It is excellent, we must all allow. Yet this government never of itself furthered any enterprise, but by the alacrity with which it got out of its way. It does not keep the country free. It does not settle the West. It does not educate. The character inherent in the American people has done all that has been accomplished; and it would have done somewhat more, if the government had not sometimes got in its way. For government is an expedient by which man would fain succeed in letting one another alone; and, as has been said, when it is most expedient, the governed are most let alone by it. Trade and commerce, if they were not made of India rubber, would never manage to bounce over the obstacles which legislators are continually putting in their way; and, if one were to judge these men wholly by the effects of their action and not partly by their intentions, they would deserve to be classed and punished with those mischievous persons who put obstructions on the railroads.

But to speak practically and as a citizen, unlike those who call themselves no-government men, I ask for, not at once no government, but at once a better government. Let every man make known what kind of government would command his respect, and that will be one step toward obtaining it.

BIBLIOGRAPHY

Pages 7-8: Tramontana, Catherine. "Repairs" in *The Best Test Preparation for the High School Proficiency Test*. Piscataway, N.J.: Research & Education Association, 1996.

Pages 10-11: Lewis, C. S. "Religion without Dogma" in *God in the Dock: Essays on Theology and Ethics*. Edited by Walter Hooper. Reprint. Grand Rapids, Mich.: Wm. B. Eerdmans Publishing Co., 1994.

Pages 116-118: Davis, Rebecca Harding. "Life in the Iron Mills." *Atlantic Monthly* 7 (1861): 430-451.

Pages 121-123: Hatfield, Mark. "Should the U.S. Constitution Be Amended to Permit School Prayer?" *The Reference Shelf: The U.S. Constitution and the Supreme Court* 60: 1 (1988) 140-4.

Pages 148-154: London, Jack. "The Story of Keesh." In *Love of Life & Other Stories*. New York: Macmillan, 1907.

Pages 157-58: Jordan, Suzanne Britt. "That Lean and Hungry Look" in *Prentice Hall Reader*. Upper Saddle River, N.J.: Prentice Hall, 2000.

Pages 195-196: Wharton, Edith. *Ethan Frome*. New York: Signet Classic, 1987.

Pages 200-202: Chopin, Kate. *Complete Works of Kate Chopin*. Baton Rouge: Louisiana State University Press, 1969.

Pages 205-206: Hazlitt, William. *Lectures on the English Poets*. Oxford University Press, 1933.

Pages 210-11: Hemingway, Ernest. *Complete Short Stories of Ernest Hemingway* (Finca Vigia edition). New York: Scribner's, 1987.

Page 214: North, Sterling. *Rascal*. New York: E. P. Dutton, 1984.

Page 215: Dickens, Charles. *A Tale of Two Cities*. New York: Signet Classic/Penguin Books USA, 1980.

Pages 216-17: Fitzgerald, F. Scott. *All the Sad Young Men*. New York: Scribner's, 1925.

Pages 218-219: Gingrich, Arnold. *The Well-Tempered Angler*. New York: New American Library Trade, 1987 (reissue edition).

Pages 221-222: Richler, Mordecai. *The Apprenticeship of Duddy Kravitz*. Toronto: Penguin Books, 1995.

Pages 224-225: Steinbeck, John. *Of Mice and Men*. New York: Bantam Books, 1988.

Page 227: Irving, Washington. "The Legend of Sleepy Hollow." In *The Sketch Book: The Legend of Sleepy Hollow and Other Stories*. New York: Signet Classic, 1990.

Pages 228-229: Lawrence, D. H. *The Complete Short Stories*. New York: Viking, 1976.

Page 234: Conrad, Joseph. *Heart of Darkness and the Secret Sharer*. New York: Bantam Books, 1981.

Page 235: Dickens, Charles. *Hard Times: A Norton Critical Edition*. New York: W. W. Norton, 1966.

Page 236: Poe, Edgar Allan. *The Works of the Late Edgar Allan Poe*. New York: J. S. Redfield, Clinton Hall, 1850.

Page 236-237: Thoreau, Henry David. *The Portable Thoreau*. Edited by Carl Bode. Reprint. New York: Viking Press, 1977.

GLOSSARY

allegory—a story in which the characters symbolize ideas or values.

alliteration—the repetition of sounds, especially at the beginnings of words.

antagonist—the person, force, or idea working against the protagonist.

antihero—a character who is pathetic rather than tragic, who does not take responsibility for his or her destructive actions.

assertion—a statement or declaration, especially one that requires evidence or explanation to be accepted as true.

autobiography—the true account of a person's life written by that person.

biography—the true account of a person's life written by someone other than that person.

blank verse—poetry in which the structure is controlled only by a metrical scheme.

characters—people created by an author to carry the action, language, and ideas of a story.

climax—the turning point or high point of action and tension in the plot.

comedy—humorous literature that has a happy ending.

commentary—literature written to explain or illuminate other works of literature or art.

conflict—a struggle or clash between two people, forces or ideas.

connotation—implied or suggested meaning.

context—the words and sentences surrounding a word or phrase that help determine the meaning of that word or phrase.

couplet—a pair of rhyming lines in poetry.

denotation—exact or dictionary meaning.

denouement—the resolution or conclusion of action.

descriptive essay—an expository essay whose primary purpose is to describe a person, place, or thing.

dialect—language that differs from the standard language in grammar, pronunciation, and idioms (natural speech versus standard English); language used by a specific group within a culture, such as a social class or ethnic group.

dialogue—the verbal exchange between two or more people; conversation.

diction—the particular choice, use, or arrangement of words.

didactic—aiming to teach or instruct (rather than entertain).

dramatic irony—in drama and fiction, when the members of the audience or readers know what more than one or more of the characters know.

exposition—the setting forth or explaining of ideas or facts; in fiction and drama, the conveyance of background information necessary to understand the plot to be developed.

falling action—the events that take place immediately after the climax in which "loose ends" are tied up.

fiction—prose literature about people, places, and events invented by the author.

figurative language—comparisons not meant to be taken literally but used for artistic effect (similes, metaphors, and personification).

foreshadowing—a suggestion or indication of things to come.

genre—a category or kind; in literature, the different categories of writing.

hyperbole—extreme exaggeration not meant to be taken literally, but done for effect.

imagery—the representation of sensory experience through language.

imagistic poem—a poem that seeks mainly to create a vivid image through language.

inference—a conclusion arrived at based upon reason, fact, or evidence.

journalism—current information and opinions expressed in newspapers, magazines, and other periodicals, as well as television and radio.

literature—something written or published that is valued for the beauty of its message, form, and emotional impact.

metaphor—a type of figurative language that compares two things by saying they are equal (e.g., your eyes are the deep blue tea).

myth—a story that attempts to explain a cultural custom, practice, belief, or natural phenomenon.

narrative essay—an expository essay whose primary purpose is to describe an experience or event.

narrator—in fiction, the person who tells the story.

non-fiction—prose literature about real people, places, and events.

novella—a very short novel or very long short story.

parable—a short, allegorical tale that illustrates a moral or religious truth.

paradox—a statement or phrase that seems to contradict itself or to conflict with common sense but which contains some truth.

parody—the imitation of a well-known work for comic effect.

personification—figurative language that endows non-human or non-animal objects with human/animal characteristics (e.g., the sun screamed down upon us).

persuasive essay—an expository essay whose primary purpose is to convince or persuade readers.

plot—the ordering of events in a story.

point of view—the perspective from which something is told or written.

protagonist—the "hero" or main character of a story; the one who faces the central conflict.

pun—a play on the meaning of a word.

reversal—in satire, when two things are switched or interchanged for effect.

rhetorical mode—how an essay is classified based upon its structure, techniques, and purpose (see descriptive essay, narrative essay, and persuasive essay).

sarcasm—sharp biting language intended to ridicule.

satire—a form of writing that exposes and ridicules its subject with the hope of bringing about change.

setting—the time and place in which a story occurs.

simile—a type of figurative language that compares two things using "like" or "as" (e.g., your eyes are as blue as the sea).

structure—the manner in which a work of literature is organized; its order of arrangement and divisions.

suspense—the state of anxiety caused by an undecided or unresolved situation.

symbol—a person, place, or object invested with special meaning to represent something else (e.g., a flag).

theme—the overall meaning or idea of a work of fiction, poetry, or drama.

thesis—the main idea of a non-fiction text.

thesis statement—the sentence(s) that express the author's thesis.

tone—the mood or attitude conveyed by writing or voice.

topic sentence—the sentence in a paragraph that expresses the main idea of that paragraph.

understatement—a statement that is deliberately restrained.

verbal irony—when the intended meaning of a word or phrase is the opposite of the expressed meaning.

voice—in non-fiction, the sound of the author speaking directly to the reader.

wit—expressing keen observations in an amusing or unusual way.

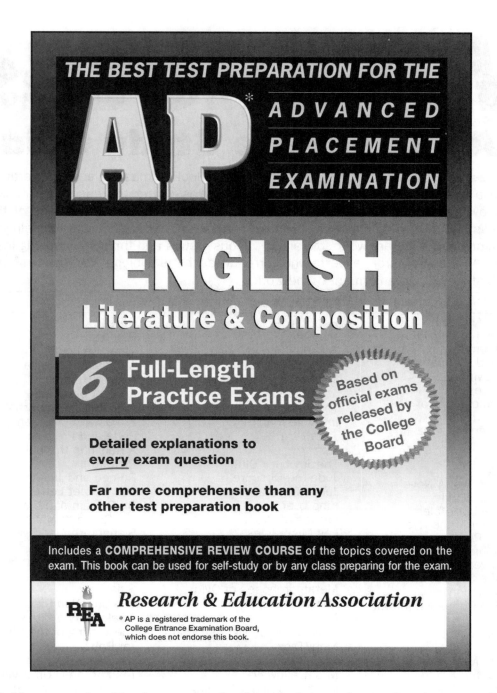

MAXnotes®
REA's Literature Study Guides

MAXnotes® are student-friendly. They offer a fresh look at masterpieces of literature, presented in a lively and interesting fashion. **MAXnotes®** offer the essentials of what you should know about the work, including outlines, explanations and discussions of the plot, character lists, analyses, and historical context. **MAXnotes®** are designed to help you think independently about literary works by raising various issues and thought-provoking ideas and questions. Written by literary experts who currently teach the subject, **MAXnotes®** enhance your understanding and enjoyment of the work.

Available **MAXnotes®** include the following:

Absalom, Absalom!
The Aeneid of Virgil
Animal Farm
Antony and Cleopatra
As I Lay Dying
As You Like It
The Autobiography of
    Malcolm X
The Awakening
Beloved
Beowulf
Billy Budd
The Bluest Eye, A Novel
Brave New World
The Canterbury Tales
The Catcher in the Rye
The Color Purple
The Crucible
Death in Venice
Death of a Salesman
Dickens Dictionary
The Divine Comedy I: Inferno
Dubliners
The Edible Woman
Emma
Euripides' Medea & Electra
Frankenstein
Gone with the Wind
The Grapes of Wrath
Great Expectations
The Great Gatsby
Gulliver's Travels
Handmaid's Tale
Hamlet
Hard Times
Heart of Darkness

Henry IV, Part I
Henry V
The House on Mango Street
Huckleberry Finn
I Know Why the Caged
    Bird Sings
The Iliad
Invisible Man
Jane Eyre
Jazz
The Joy Luck Club
Jude the Obscure
Julius Caesar
King Lear
Leaves of Grass
Les Misérables
Lord of the Flies
Macbeth
The Merchant of Venice
Metamorphoses of Ovid
Metamorphosis
Middlemarch
A Midsummer Night's Dream
Moby-Dick
Moll Flanders
Mrs. Dalloway
Much Ado About Nothing
Mules and Men
My Antonia
Native Son
1984
The Odyssey
Oedipus Trilogy
Of Mice and Men
On the Road

Othello
Paradise
Paradise Lost
A Passage to India
Plato's Republic
Portrait of a Lady
A Portrait of the Artist
    as a Young Man
Pride and Prejudice
A Raisin in the Sun
Richard II
Romeo and Juliet
The Scarlet Letter
Sir Gawain and the
    Green Knight
Slaughterhouse-Five
Song of Solomon
The Sound and the Fury
The Stranger
Sula
The Sun Also Rises
A Tale of Two Cities
The Taming of the Shrew
Tar Baby
The Tempest
Tess of the D'Urbervilles
Their Eyes Were Watching God
Things Fall Apart
To Kill a Mockingbird
To the Lighthouse
Twelfth Night
Uncle Tom's Cabin
Waiting for Godot
Wuthering Heights
Guide to Literary Terms

RESEARCH & EDUCATION ASSOCIATION
61 Ethel Road W. • Piscataway, New Jersey 08854
Phone: (732) 819-8880   **website: www.rea.com**

Please send me more information about MAXnotes®.

Name _____

Address _____

City _____ State _____ Zip _____

REA's Test Preps
The Best in Test Preparation

- REA "Test Preps" are **far more** comprehensive than any other test preparation series
- Each book contains up to **eight** full-length practice tests based on the most recent exams
- **Every** type of question likely to be given on the exams is included
- Answers are accompanied by **full** and **detailed** explanations

REA publishes over 60 Test Preparation volumes in several series. They include:

Advanced Placement Exams(APs)
Biology
Calculus AB & Calculus BC
Chemistry
Computer Science
Economics
English Language & Composition
English Literature & Composition
European History
Government & Politics
Physics B & C
Psychology
Spanish Language
Statistics
United States History

College-Level Examination Program (CLEP)
Analyzing and Interpreting Literature
College Algebra
Freshman College Composition
General Examinations
General Examinations Review
History of the United States I
History of the United States II
Human Growth and Development
Introductory Sociology
Principles of Marketing
Spanish

SAT II: Subject Tests
Biology E/M
Chemistry
English Language Proficiency Test
French
German

SAT II: Subject Tests (cont'd)
Literature
Mathematics Level IC, IIC
Physics
Spanish
United States History
Writing

Graduate Record Exams (GREs)
Biology
Chemistry
Computer Science
General
Literature in English
Mathematics
Physics
Psychology

ACT - ACT Assessment

ASVAB - Armed Services Vocational Aptitude Battery

CBEST - California Basic Educational Skills Test

CDL - Commercial Driver License Exam

CLAST - College Level Academic Skills Test

COOP & HSPT - Catholic High School Admission Tests

ELM - California State University Entry Level Mathematics Exam

FE (EIT) - Fundamentals of Engineering Exams - For both AM & PM Exams

FTCE - Florida Teacher Certification Exam

GED - High School Equivalency Diploma Exam (U.S. & Canadian editions)

GMAT CAT - Graduate Management Admission Test

LSAT - Law School Admission Test

MAT- Miller Analogies Test

MCAT - Medical College Admission Test

MTEL - Massachusetts Tests for Educator Licensure

MSAT- Multiple Subjects Assessment for Teachers

NJ HSPA - New Jersey High School Proficiency Assessment

NYSTCE: LAST & ATS-W - New York State Teacher Certification

PLT - Principles of Learning & Teaching Tests

PPST- Pre-Professional Skills Tests

PSAT - Preliminary Scholastic Assessment Test

SAT I - Reasoning Test

TExES - Texas Examinations of Educator Standards

THEA - Texas Higher Education Assessment

TOEFL - Test of English as a Foreign Language

TOEIC - Test of English for International Communication

USMLE Steps 1,2,3 - U.S. Medical Licensing Exams

U.S. Postal Exams 460 & 470

RESEARCH & EDUCATION ASSOCIATION
61 Ethel Road W. • Piscataway, New Jersey 08854
Phone: (732) 819-8880   **website: www.rea.com**

Please send me more information about your Test Prep books

Name _____

Address _____

City _____ State _____ Zip _____

REA's Test Prep Books Are The Best!

(a sample of the <u>hundreds of letters</u> REA receives each year)

" I am writing to congratulate you on preparing an exceptional study guide. In five years of teaching this course I have never encountered a more thorough, comprehensive, concise and realistic preparation for this examination. "
Teacher, Davie, FL

" I have found your publications, *The Best Test Preparation...*, to be exactly that. "
Teacher, Aptos, CA

" I used your *CLEP Introductory Sociology* book and rank it 99% — thank you! "
Student, Jerusalem, Israel

" Your *GMAT* book greatly helped me on the test. Thank you. "
Student, Oxford, OH

" I recently got the *French SAT II* Exam book from REA. I congratulate you on first-rate French practice tests. "
Instructor, Los Angeles, CA

" Your *AP English Literature and Composition* book is most impressive. "
Student, Montgomery, AL

" The REA *LSAT* Test Preparation guide is a winner! "
Instructor, Spartanburg, SC

" This book is great. Most of my friends that used the REA AP book and took the exam received 4's and 5's (mostly 5's which is the highest score! "
Student, San Jose, CA

(more on front page)